Skiing Maine

JOHN CHRISTIE
and JOSH CHRISTIE

Down East Books

Camden, Maine

Published by Down East Books
An imprint of Globe Pequot
Trade Division of The Rowman & Littlefield Publishing Group, Inc.
4501 Forbes Boulevard, Suite 200, Lanham, Maryland 20706
www.rowman.com

Unit A, Whitacre Mews, 26-34 Stannary Street, London SE11 4AB

British Library Cataloguing in Publication Information Available

Library of Congress Cataloging-in-Publication Data

Names: Christie, John, 1937-
Title: Skiing in Maine / John Christie and Josh Christie.
Description: Camden, Maine : Down East Books, [2016] | Includes index.
Identifiers: LCCN 2016012437 (print) | LCCN 2016013708 (ebook) |
ISBN
    9781608935680 (paperback) | ISBN 9781608935697 (ebook) | ISBN
    9781608935697 ()
Subjects: LCSH: Skiing—Maine—Guidebooks. | Maine—Guidebooks.
Classification: LCC GV854.5.M2 C46 2016 (print) | LCC GV854.5.M2
(ebook) |
    DDC 796.9309741—dc23
LC record available at http://lccn.loc.gov/2016012437

CONTENTS

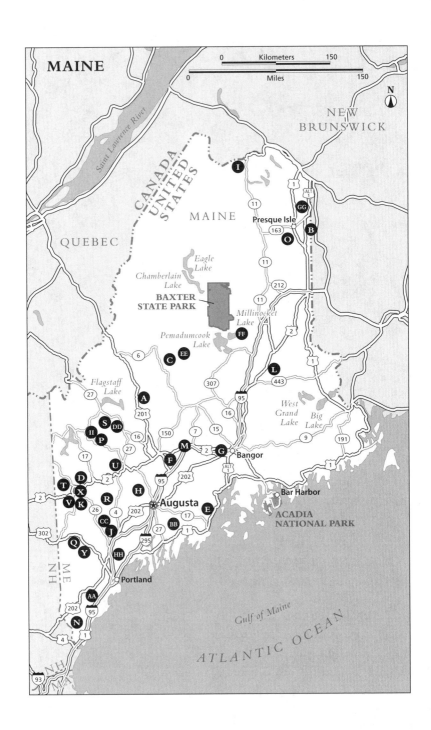

Map Key
Alpine (Downhill) Areas

- Ⓐ Baker Mountain
- Ⓑ Bigrock Mountain
- Ⓒ Big Squaw
- Ⓓ Black Mountain
- Ⓔ Camden Snow Bowl
- Ⓕ Eaton Mountain
- Ⓖ Hermon Mountain
- Ⓗ Kents Hill
- Ⓘ Lonesome Pine
- Ⓙ Lost Valley
- Ⓚ Mount Abrams
- Ⓛ Mount Jefferson
- Ⓜ Pinnacle
- Ⓝ Powder House Hill
- Ⓞ Quoggy Joe
- Ⓟ Saddleback
- Ⓠ Shawnee Peak
- Ⓡ Spruce Mountain
- Ⓢ Sugarloaf
- Ⓣ Sunday River
- Ⓤ Titcomb Mountain

Nordic (Cross-country) Areas

- Ⓥ Bethel Nordic Ski Center
- Ⓓ Black Mountain
- Ⓧ Carter's Cross-Country Center
- Ⓨ Five Fields Farm
- Ⓘ Fort Kent Outdoor Center
- ⒶⒶ Harris Farm Cross-Country Center
- ⒷⒷ Hidden Valley Nature Center
- ⒸⒸ Carter's Cross Country Ski Center
- Ⓙ Lost Valley Touring Center
- ⒹⒹ Maine Huts and Trails
- ⒺⒺ Maine Wilderness Lodges
- Ⓕ New England Outdoor Center
- ⒼⒼ Nordic Heritage Center
- ⒽⒽ Pineland Farms
- Ⓘ Rangeley Lakes Trail Center
- Ⓡ Spruce Mountain
- Ⓢ Sugarloaf Outdoor Center
- Ⓤ Titcomb Mountain Nordic

SKIING MAINE: A HISTORY

The story of skiing in Maine and its growth into a winter pastime is a fascinating tale that demonstrates how at least three uniquely different cultures can unwittingly combine to change the face of a state and an industry. Scandinavians who populated Aroostook County in the nineteenth century, French Canadians who worked in the mills along the Kennebec and Androscoggin Rivers, and ingenious Yankee farmers all contributed in their special ways to the birth and growth of both a sport and an industry.

The Scandinavians first used Nordic skis to get around their farms in the winter, then began to use them for recreational purposes and ultimately for competition. The Francos focused on both cross-country and jumping disciplines and went on to develop internationally acclaimed competitors. And the Yankees put old pickup trucks up on blocks, ran a rope around a rear wheel, and dragged local kids up pasture hillsides.

But that was just the beginning. In less than a century, these early faltering footsteps would lay the foundation for a sport that would capture the imagination of both the state and the nation, and turn rural communities into winter destinations.

The Swedish Invasion

The first recorded skiing activity in Maine was in Aroostook County during the winter of 1870–71, when long wooden skis of Scandinavian origin were introduced as the best way to get around in deep snow. Granted, Native Americans and Maine trappers and hunters had been using snowshoes for centuries, but skis offered a better alternative for covering long distances rapidly.

Some twenty years prior to that, the Maine legislature was looking for ways to populate the vast and nearly uncharted northern third of the state. The legislature knew that homesteading in the great north Maine woods would appeal to only a select and hardy few, so they sweetened the pot by offering free land to those who would take up the challenge.

In the Thoreauvian words of Widgery Thomas, Maine state legislator and former US ambassador to Sweden:

> Before 1870, the primeval forest covered all the land, stretching way over hill and dale as far as the eye could reach. No habitation of civilized man had ever been erected in these vast northern woods; through their branches the smoke from a settler's cabin had never curled; in their depths the blows from a settler's ax had never resounded. Here roamed the moose and prowled the bear, and here the silence of midnight was broken by the hooting of the arctic owl.

But Thomas knew well, as he called the Scandinavians, "the tall, stout, hardy race of Northmen, inured to hardship, patient of labor, economical, religious and honest" who populated Scandinavia in general, and specifically Sweden.

So, with the approval of the legislature, he sailed for Sweden in May of 1870 to offer a 100-acre parcel to any Swede willing to settle in Maine. Some two months later he returned with twenty-two men, eleven women, and eighteen children to a spot deep in the woods north of Caribou, and New Sweden was born.

For $1 a day, the new arrivals cut roads and built log camps. Garden spots were cleared of trees, stumps, and rocks, and turnips, winter wheat, and rye were planted.

The new arrivals were accustomed to cold weather and deep snow, and they safely and comfortably endured their first winter as Americans and Mainers. In fact, there's no record of a single day of illness in the camp.

One reason they were able to both survive and get around outside was their knowledge of how to build and use skis from their native land.

The skis they made from local ash and maple trees were long and, inspired by their Scandinavian forebears, unequal in length. Although the traditional pair from their homeland had a great disparity between the gliding ski and the pushing ski (imagine riding a scooter), the New Sweden skis were more equal in length, with the long one being about 10 feet long and the shorter only about 6 inches shorter.

Their skis were secured to their boots with only a leather toe loop and had distinctive tips that were curled up, giving the appearance of a Viking ship. And every ski maker added his own distinctive markings. Skis were used to get around for daily chores, for the kids to get to school, and for wives to head to town for necessary goods.

French Fliers

In the early twentieth century, French Canadian immigrants began to make their indelible mark on Maine skiing along the banks of the Kennebec and Androscoggin Rivers. Starting in the 1920s, lads who worked in the paper mill in Rumford stretched their ski legs at what was called the Spruce Street Area, a short walking distance out of town. They honed their nascent Alpine skills on rudimentary gear, and in spite of the gear, they became hooked. In their hearts though, they were ski jumpers through and through.

They built a jump to hone their technique in Spruce, which served them well until its collapse in 1942. Aurele Legere won the Eastern Ski Jumping Championship in 1936, establishing the boys from the Rumford area as formidable Nordic jumpers. And since many of the established competitions required that one enter both jumping and cross-country events, they began to train for, and excel in, cross-country as well.

After World War II the paper-mill workers built a new jump at Scotty's Mountain, an imposing structure on which was recorded a jump of 202 feet. Additionally, the end of the war saw the return of local boys who had served with distinction in the famed 10th Mountain Division, having trained in the Rockies and fought in Italy.

The final section of this book, "Notable Maine Skiers," records the achievements of many men and women from this corner of Maine who contributed to the history of the sport.

Yankee Ingenuity

During the 1920s and 1930s, winter carnivals were staged in communities as disparate as Portland, Fort Fairfield, and Greenville. They were *the* events that helped residents not only endure but enjoy the long Maine winters. Folks from Bangor packed the cars of the Bangor and Aroostook Railroad to participate and enjoy the spectacle of the carnival in Greenville.

Competitions, dances, and all manner of celebratory events were staged at these midwinter festivals, and thousands participated. Once, on the banks of the Kennebec River in Waterville, spectators stood ten rows deep just to watch a few brave skiers slide down the hill. On February 3, 1935, the first of many so-called Snow Trains pulled out of the station in Portland, bound for Fryeburg with 229 enthusiasts aboard.

The success of the Snow Train in 1935 convinced the Fryeburg Winter Sports Committee to seriously consider what they might do the next year to bring even more people to the sleepy little western Maine town in the winter.

Directly behind the railroad station stood Starks Hill, and some energetic citizens cut two ski trails that offered advanced terrain for brave skiing neophytes.

On nearby Jockey Cap wooden toboggan chutes were constructed, followed by the installation of Maine's first uphill transportation device, a rope tow funded by ten enterprising young residents who each ponied up $25. Skiers and curious spectators flocked to the new ski area.

Just two weeks later folks in nearby Bridgton, not wanting to be left out of the new fad and tired of trudging up the fairways of the golf course at Bridgton Highlands to try their hands at skiing, installed Maine's second rope tow. A scant two years later, after a racing trail had been cut on Pleasant Mountain, west of Bridgton, the rope tow was moved there from Bridgton Highlands to serve an open slope at the bottom of the trail. Inspired by the apparent success of Cranmore Mountain, a major ski facility in North Conway, New Hampshire, funded by local boy and Bowdoin graduate Harvey Dow Gibson, these early Maine skiing pioneers in Bridgton sought to get in on the emerging craze and did so with gusto.

Maine's first chairlift was installed on Pleasant Mountain a short time later. Simultaneously in towns all over the state, from Fort Kent to Berwick and dozens of towns in between, rope tows began to dot the hillsides of once silent Maine communities and instead echoed with the laughter of delighted youths and adults skiing for the first time.

Not only did ingenious and self-taught Yankee engineers figure out how to build and operate rudimentary rope tows, they also began to experiment with other possible uphill transport devices and to search for new mountains to build ski areas.

In the late 1940s political movers and shakers in Augusta recognized that perhaps ski area development could be a part of Maine's economic development future. This notion gained traction when Governor Horace Hildreth charged his Maine Development Commission with the task of calling together representatives of several ski clubs, operating in various parts of the state, to learn how to expand the state's winter tourism business.

Out of that first meeting was born the Maine Ski Council, which at its inaugural meeting formed an Area Development Committee to "look over all of those mountains in Maine which Maine skiers deemed as developable and determine which of these could be most feasibly turned into a ski area."

Their attention was drawn to Sugarloaf Mountain northwest of Kingfield, where Amos Winter, a local general-store owner, had cut a trail with the help of some locals and other interested skiers from around the state. A visit in 1948 convinced the group that skiing could be an important economic endeavor for Maine along the northern flank of this awe-inspiring 4,000-foot mountain.

In the two decades that followed, ski area development and expansion exploded, thanks in great part to a mere handful of pioneers with the energy, guts, and imagination to create a new industry and to stand at the forefront of technological innovation. Here are a few that stand out:

Donald, Norton, and Stuart Cross

In Locke Mills, south of Bethel, in the mid-twentieth century, the three Cross brothers owned a family woodlot on Mount Abram, and from that lot, among others, they derived their living as timber harvesters. One day Norton Cross was looking down from the top at a cutting on the north side of the mountain and realized that they had opened up a perfect ski trail on some very inviting terrain. At the same time, the brothers were seeing others become financially successful in the ski business. Since the brothers liked to ski themselves and they saw a developing marketplace, they decided to build their own ski area.

But their real contribution to the sport and the business was their uncanny ability to translate their farming and logging experience into innovative methods of snow grooming that transcended everything available and around the ski business.

They modified farm implements to scarify ice and hard-packed snow; they transported snow from the woods and the parking lots to cover thin or bare spots on the trails; and they experimented with devices to mix compressed air and water to manufacture snow.

All of their innovations derived from an innate marketing ability, a quality one might not necessarily associate with rural Maine natives. Every technological move they made was with one goal in mind: Provide the customer with the best possible skiing experience.

Otto Wallingford

In the 1960s this Auburn apple grower often stood on his hillside of native fruit trees and looked down the gentle slope, his farm within a few minutes of Lewiston and Auburn, two bustling Androscoggin River communities. Otto Wallingford's idea of turning the area into what would become one of Maine's best incubators for budding recreational and competitive skiers was only half of his genius.

An engineering graduate from the University of Maine, Wallingford quickly turned his problem-solving acumen into inventions that captured the imagination of other ski area operators and changed the worlds of snow grooming and snowmaking.

His patented Powder Maker was a first-of-a-kind improvement in working eastern hardpack into skiable fluff; his elevated snow guns produced more snow, more efficiently and of higher quality, than any seen up to that point in the industry; and as an importer and distributor of European snow-grooming devices, he single-handedly changed the American skiing landscape.

Robert "Bunny" Bass

A third-generation shoemaker in Wilton, Robert Bass was also an avid skier. He convinced the rest of his family that they should begin producing leather boots specifically designed for skiing at their already-busy factory. Although the company began making ski boots prior to World War II, the demand for leather wartime gear cut short the continuation of that product line.

Directly following the war, however, the company reemerged as one of the country's leading ski boot manufacturers, constantly introducing innovative improvements. During the 1960s Bass began importing plastic Swiss ski boots, nimbly keeping pace with customer tastes and preferences.

The Ski Boom

During the 1960s skiing, both as a sport and a business, was growing exponentially nationwide. And Maine was happily participating in the phenomenon. New ski areas were being built while, and at the same time and for a variety of reasons, dozens of small, rope tow–served community hills ceased operations. Of the once more than eighty such slopes, only a couple operate to this day.

Some of the major projects launched in the 1960s and 1970s came to unhappy ends, but the industry today is flourishing, as the following section clearly demonstrates.

Note: Prices reflect the 2015–2016 season rates. Check with individual ski areas for most current costs.

Alpine (downhill) Areas

BAKER MOUNTAIN

This quirky throwback to ski days of yore operates on natural snow on winter weekends and school vacation weeks through the generosity of the local communities and volunteers from the Baker Mountain Ski Tow Club. Season pass holders also volunteer their time to make sure this archetypical community slope can continue operating and introducing new skiers and boarders to the wonders of winter.

There are even enough lights strategically placed along the side of this 460-vertical-foot mountain to allow night skiing when conditions permit.

Visitors will find two beginner and three intermediate trails. One gains access to these trails on a clunky but dependable T-bar that was installed in 1969 to replace the original rope tows installed prior to 1940. Lift tickets are still under 10 bucks and make this one of the best deals going.

The original area was the brainchild of Allen Quimby Jr., a local veneer mill owner and operator who loved to ski and wanted his family and other locals to have an easily accessible ski slope of their own.

During the school vacation week in February, kids are provided with free lessons. Although the area is adored by local devotees, visitors from far away are made to feel welcome in the 1940s-style base lodge where generations of locals and others warmed themselves in front of the fire between runs.

You'll find the area in the town of Moscow, just north of Bingham on well-traveled and -maintained US 201, the preferred route for Mainers to get to Quebec City.

But a word of warning: Known as "Moose Alley," this road is notorious for encounters with this ungainly, and sometimes lethal, member of the deer family.

Location: Moscow
Contact: (207) 717-0404
Price range: Adults (including seniors) and children $9
Number of trails: 5
Difficulty ratings: 2 beginner, 3 intermediate
Lifts: 1 T-bar
Snowmaking: None
Website: None

BIGROCK MOUNTAIN

M ars Hill towers over the surrounding Aroostook County potato fields. Shortly after Alaska and Hawaii became the forty-ninth and fiftieth states, the local Junior Chamber of Commerce did what they thought to be most logical for their area: build a ski area so county folks, along with their neighbors in New Brunswick, Canada, would have a place to enjoy the long northern Maine winters. So, with Wendell Pierce supplying both the energy and the money, development began.

In the years following that auspicious launch in 1960, the area continued to provide exceptional skiing on the 980-vertical-foot mountain for folks as far away as Bangor, Maine, and Fredericton, New Brunswick, each about 2 hours away.

Forty years later enter the Portland-based Libra Foundation, in 2000, which funded a newly formed entity, the Maine Winter Sports Center. Operating as Bigrock Mountain, significant capital investment turned the somewhat moribund facility into a thriving destination.

Now sporting a triple chair as well as a double, along with a Poma, a handle lift, and a carpet, there is plenty of uphill capacity for the biggest weekend crowds.

With fourteen intermediate, five beginner, and ten advanced trails, there is enough variety for skiers of every ability. A terrain park with twenty elements keeps boarders entertained, and an extensive snowmaking system serves to cover some 80 percent of the mountain's terrain with man-made snow when nature fails to cooperate. But using fake snow is rare up in Maine's far north country, where snowfall totals are legendary.

Among the many appeals at Bigrock is an enticing ticket-pricing structure that allows adults ages 18 through 64 to ski for just 22 bucks a day on weekdays and 38 on weekends and during holiday weeks. For folks in the 65-to-74 age group and kids, it's even cheaper. And if you're 75 or older, you ski as a guest of the area.

Similarly reasonable season-pass rates are also available, as are lessons for both skiers and boarders.

Lift tickets are even more reasonable than at many other areas because thirteen of the trails are lighted, so your day can extend well past sunset. A single-day ticket (comparably priced to many similar areas) buys you about 4 extra hours of skiing at the end of the day.

In 2014, after making significant capital investments, modernizing and operating the area for fourteen years, the Libra Foundation generously turned the mountain over to the community, thus completing the circle that started over half a century ago.

There are many different kinds of ski-and-stay packages at nearby inns and cabins that combine lodging with lift tickets and meals at the ski area. The Hampton Inn in Presque Isle even includes breakfast for two at their facility as part of the package.

Reasonably priced packages can be found at My Sunset Cabins in Mars Hill, Blaine Country Cabins in Blaine, the Bear Paw Inn in Mars Hill, and the Presque Isle Inn and Convention Center.

Bear in mind that Bigrock is closed on Monday and Tuesday, except during vacation weeks, so plan your visit accordingly.

Location: 37 Graves Hill Rd., Mars Hill
Contact: (207) 425-6711
Price range: Adults $38, children $17, seniors $27
Number of trails: 29
Difficulty ratings: 5 beginner, 14 intermediate, 10 advanced
Lifts: 1 triple, 1 double, 1 handle, 1 Poma, 1 carpet
Snowmaking: 80%
Website: www.bigrockmaine.com

BIG SQUAW

Squaw Mountain, just west of Greenville on the scenic road over to Jackman, has had an interesting and somewhat peripatetic past.

This area was first developed in the 1960s by a devoted group of Piscataquis County business leaders who wanted to increase winter traffic in the Greenville area and provide recreation for interested winter sports enthusiasts in the region. Over the years the area has gone through a series of ownerships and management (including both Scott Paper Company and the Maine Department of Conservation), culminating with the current dedicated effort of community members to keep the place operating. There is even an effort now underway by volunteers to not only continue operating the facility but to replace the long-dormant and condemned double chair to the top of the mountain. This new lift will once again allow skiers and boarders renewed access to the outstanding terrain that was enjoyed for several decades by loyal Squaw Mountain aficionados.

Legendary ski trail designer Sel Hannah, of Franconia, New Hampshire, undertook the task to lay out the first ski trails on the nearly 4,000-foot Squaw Mountain, which looked down upon nearby Moosehead Lake.

Although he was credited in his career for designing more than 300 ski areas in North America, he once said, in response to a question about his favorite trail out of the thousands he had been responsible for laying out, "The Penobscot Trail at Squaw Mountain in Greenville, Maine, is it. The views from the top of the trail are just wonderful. Once you start skiing down, the trail moves with the terrain of the mountain better than any other I've seen. There is a variety of sharp turns and wide round turns—the pattern is constantly changing. Rolls in the trail are a challenge if you ski them fast, yet by sweeping around them the novice can ski comfortably. The Penobscot is a fun trail for skiers of all abilities."

That's the good news. The bad news is that the old double chair that gives you access to this treasure has not operated since an accident rendered it unusable several years ago. Ambitious skiers and boarders can be seen climbing up from the top of the currently operating triple to still take turns and, equally important, enjoy the spectacular view north over Moosehead Lake, with Katahdin looming on the near horizon.

But rumor has it that a local effort to find a replacement, perhaps a used chair from a Vermont ski area, is gaining traction.

Notwithstanding the absence of a lift to the summit, there is still some delightful skiing on the lower 680-vertical-foot terrain accessed by the still-operating triple, thanks to the Friends of Big Squaw Mountain, a nonprofit organization that was founded, in its words, "to promote, preserve and protect the future of downhill skiing and racing at Big Squaw Mountain."

Even from the top of this lower terrain, the views are nothing short of breathtaking. The refurbished lodge at the base has a snack bar and grill that serves up traditional skiing comfort food, along with hot soups and specials, appreciated by visitors who brave the sometimes brutal temps of the north Maine woods.

Two novice, eleven intermediate, and an expert trail (directly under the triple for show-offs) provide plenty of variety and easy cruising. One trail even leads you down around the base of the old double, with its adjacent base lodge and hotel. On this trail you can visualize what the place might be like if the momentum to once again gain access to the top continues.

Locals operate a groomer and a modest snowmaking system, as well as a ski school. In recent years new glades have been created for tree-loving explorers.

The area has recently been open Friday through Sunday only, in addition to school vacation weeks, but you are urged to call or check their website before planning your trip to get their current operating schedule.

Rates are hard to beat: Adult tickets are $25, while children in kindergarten through grade 12 ski for $20. Kids under 5 and codgers over 70 get lift tickets for free.

There are over a dozen inns, motels, and sporting camps in the area open all winter (catering to throngs of snowmobilers who frequent the region), and plenty of restaurants and bars for local food specialties and libations.

Location: 447 Ski Resort Rd., Big Moose Township
Contact: (207) 695-2400
Price range: Adults $25, children $20, kids under 5 and seniors 70+ free
Number of trails: 14
Difficulty ratings: 2 beginner, 11 intermediate, 1 advanced
Lifts: 1 triple
Snowmaking: None
Website: www.skibigsquaw.com

BLACK MOUNTAIN

Though Black Mountain (in Rumford, not to be confused with New Hampshire's Black Mountain) was opened in the 1960s, its history dates back to before World War II. The legendary Chisolm Ski Club, which produced Olympians Chummy Broomhall, Jack Lufkin, Robert Pidacks, Frank Lutick Jr., and Jim Miller, was founded in Rumford in 1924. The group built a ski jump off of Spruce Street at the time and went on to add a rope tow. Following World War II the group built a ski jump on nearby Scotty's Mountain, along with a rope tow, before moving the whole enterprise to 450 acres on Black Mountain, the area's current home.

In the intervening decades a lodge and Nordic network were built around Black Mountain. A T-bar was also installed, though it only climbed partway up the slope. A planned summit lift wouldn't be installed until the early twenty-first century.

In recent years Black has seen a number of upgrades: a triple chair, a double chair, and a free handle tow in the beginner's area now supplement the original lift, and the triple rises nearly 1,100 vertical feet, providing access to more than fifteen wonderfully groomed trails.

All of these improvements were the result of the Maine Winter Sports Center's acquisition of the area in 2004, with the support of a grant from the Libra Foundation. Though that relationship ended in 2014, a community organization raised funds to take over operations of Black Mountain; the area itself was donated to the group by Maine Winter Sports and the Libra Foundation.

Some three-quarters of the terrain is covered with man-made snow when necessary. But with an average annual snowfall of over 120 inches, Black Mountain gets its fair share of Mother Nature's generosity.

Along with the Alpine skiing, there is a tubing park and a network of cross-country trails.

A full-day ticket (9 a.m. to 4 p.m. Saturday or Sunday) is $29 for adults, $25 for kids ages 6 through 17, and $25 for the 62-to-74 category. After that it's free, as it is for kids 5 and under. And to encourage any Maine student in kindergarten up to second grade to take up skiing and snowboarding, season passes for that age group are free! There's night skiing, summit to base, from 6 to 9 p.m. on Friday nights for an additional $4 added to the regular Friday rate of just $10. There's even a bar in the base lodge for après ski.

Location: 39 Glover Rd., Rumford
Contact: (207) 364-8977
Price range: Adults $29, children $25, seniors 75+ free
Number of trails: 35
Difficulty ratings: 5 beginner, 15 intermediate, 15 advanced
Lifts: 1 triple, 1 double, 1 T-bar, 2 handle tow
Snowmaking: 90%
Website: www.skiblackmountain.org

CAMDEN SNOW BOWL

Just west of the beautiful town of Camden, and overlooking Penobscot Bay, the town-owned Snow Bowl stands as the perfect example of how public and private interests can be conjoined for the benefit of all. Both public and private sectors sustain not only the operations of a local hill, but they work to develop the facilities in such a way that the entire ski experience can compare favorably with what one will find at a major resort. Far from competing with its bigger brethren, the Snow Bowl will help ensure a continuing supply of new entrants into the sport, for the benefit of all.

A mecca for midcoast skiers for some three-quarters of a century, the nearly 1,000-vertical-foot terrain on Ragged Mountain has bred and happily satisfied generations of Alpine enthusiasts, beginning with a modest rope tow installed by the Civilian Conservation Corps in the late 1930s. It now stands as one of only two ski areas in Maine started before the Second World War still operating today, and it's the only one bearing its original name. The other, now Shawnee Peak, began its life and operated for years as Pleasant Mountain.

Over the years, the facility, like all ski areas, public and private, has suffered the industry challenge of maintaining the facility and simultaneously continuing to improve the experience for its users. In 2015 the Camden Snow Bowl embarked on the first phase of a two-year improvement project that stands as the most dramatic and expensive, at $6.5 million, development at any ski area at that time in the state of Maine (and perhaps New England), bar none.

The entire redevelopment project marks the culmination of five years hard work by the citizen-constituted Ragged Mountain Recreation Area Foundation and a town-appointed Redevelopment Committee, not to mention town administrators, Snow Bowl staff, and, perhaps most important, Camden voters who overwhelmingly approved a $2 million bond issue in the fall of 2013.

The Capital Campaign Committee of the foundation successfully garnered the necessary $4.5 million in private commitments to trigger the municipality's acceptance of the responsibility to fund the project balance.

Near the top of the unloading area for the "new" triple chair (which old Pleasant Mountain skiers will recognize as the original triple there), at about the same elevation as the top of the long T-bar that it replaced, blasting created a skier-friendly unloading area. The small T-bar being replaced by the double chair has always been a problem to ride and master for first-timers, so the new beginner area may, in the long run, prove to be one of the most important elements of the redevelopment. Additional ledge blasting and removal along the lift line helped shape the terrain for improved skiability, and also provided fill material to level out some problem areas.

One added benefit of blasting the terrain at the top is that the heretofore spectacular view of Camden and Penobscot Bay has been even further enhanced.

Even the previously intimidating steep slope in front of the base lodge has been creatively recontoured into a smoother transition between slope segments and is now a visually enticing and inviting area for first-timers and neophytes, with a great location for spectating along the lodge's deck.

In past years all of the terrain served by snowmaking off the short T-bar was to the west of the lift, with no novice terrain easily accessible. Major recontouring and shaping of the Coaster trail to the east of the lift will now provide an easy and inviting opportunity for first-timers to descend to the base area.

Before the renovation, only about 45 percent of the skiable terrain at the area benefited from man-made snow, which has now been doubled to over 80 percent. The importance of this capability to a ski area, especially along Maine's coastal plain, where temperatures, humidity, and modest natural snowfall conspire to make ski operations difficult at best, cannot be overstated. History has shown that without snowmaking, the Snow Bowl would probably not have survived to this point. But the ability and capacity to make snow, along with recent technological improvements in the equipment, virtually assures continuous skiing from opening until closing day. This assurance is one of the reasons the community stepped up so generously and confidently to help fund the bold redevelopment project.

Forty-six high-efficiency snow guns have been added to the system, thanks to substantial incentives from Efficiency Maine. Additionally, a second 400-horsepower water pump has virtually doubled the rate at which snow can be made.

New lights for expanded night operations now assure top-to-bottom post-sunset skiing, and modern LED fixtures are projected to consume about half the power of the bulbs they replaced.

Congestion has been alleviated by a considerable degree as the rental shop, ticket sales, and ski-and-ride school desk are now relocated in a new, temporary building abutting the east side of the lodge, immediately accessible off the deck in the front. During especially busy times, lift tickets will also be sold from a window facing the deck.

The summer of 2017 will see the construction of a new, $2.5 million base lodge that will once again consolidate all skier services.

With an increase in the skiable terrain by 35 percent, night skiing terrain up 50 percent, lift capacity increased by 64 percent (100 percent to the summit), and snowmaking capability increased by 100 percent, the Snow Bowl now promises a very different experience for skiers and boarders than in the past. By increasing the uphill capacity of the lifts alone (including the new carpet conveyor), from the previous 2,125 people per hour to some 3,300 people per hour, the facility has taken the necessary steps to ensure that more people than ever can enjoy and appreciate this midcoast treasure.

Skiers familiar with the Snow Bowl will have a hard time recognizing the terrain when they pay their first visit to the Snow Bowl after all of the improvements, and first-timers are in for a pleasant surprise.

The lower nine towers and both terminals of the old double chairlift have been moved and reinstalled at a point paralleling the old short T-bar, and terminate slightly higher up the mountain on a welcoming, beginner-friendly plateau. This responds to what has historically been the Snow Bowl's principal shortcoming: easy terrain within clear view of the base area that beckons beginners anxious to test their skiing skills. In prior years it was a long leap from the little handle lift on the nearly flat terrain at the bottom of the steep slope in front of the lodge to the chair taking them to a point much higher up on the mountain.

Snacks and hot beverages are available, at very reasonable prices, in a base lodge snack bar. Try the grilled-cheese-and-bacon sandwich, and add a generous order of hand-cut fries for a satisfying lunch.

A wide choice of hotels, motels, inns, and bed-and-breakfasts is available in Camden and adjacent Rockport and Rockland, and many restaurants and pubs are now open year-round.

Rates at the town-owned ski area reflect a commitment to make weekday skiing and boarding as affordable as possible at just $27 for adults for all day, or 2 hours for $20, $24 for students, and just $10 for everyone over the age of 70.

Location: 20 Barnestown Rd., Camden
Contact: (207) 236-3438
Price range: Adults $39, children and seniors $34, weekends
Number of trails: 23
Difficulty ratings: 2 beginner, 8 intermediate, 13 advanced
Lifts: 1 triple chair, 1 double chair, 1 conveyer carpet
Snowmaking: 80%
Website: www.camdensnowbowl.com

EATON MOUNTAIN

Back in the 1920s a few locals were climbing up Eaton Mountain in Skowhegan to try their hand at skiing, and by the 1930s they had hacked out two trails from the top to the bottom.

But it was in the late 1950s that Paul Sylvain took the leap and started to actually develop a ski area on the imposing little hill about 5 minutes east of town on US 2. He bought the land, cut three trails, built a base lodge, and installed a rope tow, ready for the winter of 1961–62.

It became a mecca for central Maine skiers warming up for the larger mountains to the west. Over the years development at Eaton Mountain continued, culminating with the installation of a double chair.

The area fell on hard times in the 1970s, and operations ultimately ceased some years later, until Dave Beers bought the place and began its rejuvenation. He first turned the area into a snow-tubing park and then, in the winter of 2014–15, finally reopened it for skiing on the lower part of the hill only. But his energetic plans call for eventually replacing or completely overhauling the existing chairlift.

For its reopening as a ski area and tubing facility, the 525-foot mountain featured two new tows: a 700-foot-long handle tow that serves 125 vertical feet of intermediate terrain along with a small terrain park with jumps and full-size rails; and a beginner rope tow running 330 feet from the base lodge on a protected beginner slope.

Once the chairlift is reopened, the existing network of a dozen trails, ranging from novice to expert, will once again echo with the sounds of happy skiers and boarders who've waited years for the rebirth of this local favorite.

Plans for improving the facility prior to the new lift to the top include a 800-foot handle tow to service a widened trail on which there will be lights for night skiing and tools for snowmaking.

Once the chairlift is reactivated, there are plans to install both lights and snowmaking from the summit.

Skis, ski boots, snowboards, and helmets are available for rent, and beginner ski and snowboard lessons are offered.

Location: 89 Lambert Rd., Skowhegan
Contact: (207) 474-2666
Price range: Adults, children, and seniors $15
Number of trails: 15
Difficulty ratings: 4 beginner, 5 intermediate, 6 advanced
Lifts: 2 handle tows
Snowmaking: None
Website: www.eatonmountain.com

HERMON MOUNTAIN

G ood people, good times, good skiing, good food."
Hermon Mountain's motto speaks to their devotion to
being a family-friendly community hill, easily accessible to beginners
and experts alike. Located in Hermon, just about 10 minutes from
Bangor, this mountain offers a variety of terrain accessed by a handful of lifts.

Over fifty years ago Bernard Jackson was doing some logging on
a hillside behind his house and realized that if he opened up his tote
roads a little more, he and his son, Bernard Jr., could do some skiing
on the small mountain just out his back door.

Hermon first opened in the early 1960s, home to a single rope
tow and operated by the Jackson family. It grew quickly in the heady
days of the '60s, buoyed by the national interest in skiing and growth
of the ski business around the country. A T-bar running from the base
to the summit was installed in the late '60s, and another was added a
few years later to access beginner terrain. Hermon's growth was sty-
mied when a fire took out the base lodge in 1981, followed by nearly
half a decade of snowless winters. Growth picked up a bit at the turn
of the century, and they installed a double chairlift (their first nonsur-
face lift) leading to the mountain and an expanded lodge.

Today, Hermon's three lifts service twenty trails (evenly split
between beginner, intermediate, and advanced terrain) on 350 vertical feet. And skiers need not fear snowless winters like those in the
1980s. Hermon now boasts 100 percent snowmaking for their small
hill. Night skiing until 9 p.m. during the workweek makes the ski
area a hit with local after-school programs, as well as skiers who want
to get in a few turns after a day in the office.

The trails at Hermon spread skiers out pretty widely (or as widely
as possible, given their small size), with easier trails in the center of the
hill and expert trails on the margins. The toughest trails at Hermon
are on the southern edge, where the narrow black diamonds Snake

and Jammer offer some legitimate thrills. Scenic and Lakeview, both directly above the lodge, live up to their names, with great views of Hermon Pond. Moving north, short shots like Mini Heat and Cyclone provide some short, steep drops.

The comfy base lodge has all the requisite amenities, and the snack bar has a wide variety of traditional slope-side offerings. If you're into pizza, you've got to try a slice. The base lodge even offers video games for the kids.

Adult tickets are just $27, and half-day and evenings are $22. A tubing slope north of the lodge is also an option for visitors, with tickets priced at $12.

Location: 441 Newburg Rd., Hermon
Contact: (207) 848-5192
Price range: Adults (including seniors) $27, children $22
Number of trails: 20
Difficulty ratings: 6 beginner, 7 intermediate, 7 advanced
Lifts: 1 double, 1 T-bar, 1 handle tow
Snowmaking: 100%
Website: www.skihermonmountain.com

KENTS HILL

First opened in the early 1950s by the Kents Hill School as a training facility for its skiers, this venerable throwback to older times has a rope tow that might make a claim to be the fastest one in the world still in operation.

In the 1980s snowmaking, lights for night use, and a groomer were all added, and the area continues to this day to fulfill its original mission.

Along with digital race-timing equipment, the area has a lodge with a ski-tuning room, equipment storage area, a reception room and a meeting room with a fireplace and a kitchen, and a deck that looks out on one of the grandest views in the entire area. As of the 2015 season, a second beginner rope tow has been installed.

The school and the ski area are a few miles west of Augusta, Maine's capital city.

Public use is limited to a local club for youngsters that charges $300 for two nights per week during the season from 6 to 8 p.m.

Location: 39 Chimney Rd., Readfield
Contact: (207) 685-9061
Price range: adults , children, seniors $300 a season, local ski club only
Lifts: 2 rope tows
Snowmaking: Limited
Website: www.kentshill.org

LONESOME PINE

Holding the record as the northernmost ski area in Maine, Lonesome Pine's 500-vertical-foot hill looms just south of downtown Fort Kent on the Madawaska River. Its location attracts skiers and boarders from two countries, with Canadian visitors helping sustain the member-owned, nonprofit facility. The volunteer workforce supplies the necessary labor to keep things humming along.

In fact, the adult day ticket, at $22, is listed on the rate board as the same as a membership fee, as is the $15 half-day and evening rate. College and other students ski for $17 all day and $13 for a half day or evening.

Uphill transport is provided for beginners on a handle tow, and once having mastered that hill, skiers and boarders graduate to the T-bar, for both day and night use.

One novice, seven intermediate, and five expert trails provide plenty of variety, and the area's location often offers better natural-snow skiing than those farther to the south. Their grooming is a matter of pride, and they have both the equipment and the skilled operators necessary.

Night skiing is available on Friday, as the mountain operates from 3 to 9 p.m., and on Saturday and Sunday it runs from 9 a.m. to 4 p.m. The ski area is closed Monday through Thursday, except during school vacation weeks.

Location: Forest Avenue, Fort Kent
Contact: (207) 834-5202
Price range: Adults (including seniors) $22, children $17
Number of trails: 13
Difficulty ratings: 1 beginner, 7 intermediate, 5 advanced
Lifts: 1 T-bar, 1 J-bar
Snowmaking: 60%
Website: www.lonesomepines.org

LOST VALLEY

Auburn's Lost Valley is the quintessential family ski area. From the convenient location (less than an hour from Portland) to the Technicolor chairlift to the gentle slopes and family-friendly lodge, it is a paradise for beginning skiers. Even the expert slopes, while not as challenging as their neighbors in the western mountains, offer some easy thrills.

As is often the case with community ski areas, there is more to Lost Valley than meets the eye. Certainly, it is a great place for families and beginning skiers of all ages. Dig a bit deeper into the history of the Auburn slopes, and you'll find that Olympians and pioneers also came from the 240-foot hill.

Lost Valley was founded in 1961 by Otto Wallingford and Camille Gardner. Wallingford, an orchardist, found himself bored during the winter months. He partnered with Gardner, whose land was adjacent to his, to open the little community ski area.

The area opened in the winter of 1961, serviced by a single rope tow. A T-bar was installed the following year, and the mountain's first chairlift was installed three years later. A second double chairlift was installed in 1971, and a few more trails were cut. Aside from a handful of improvements and minor changes, the Lost Valley of the early 1970s—aside from a couple fixed lifts that service just over a dozen trails—is strikingly similar to the one you will find today.

Lost Valley's lasting impact on the ski industry came from Wallingford's inventive nature. At the family orchard, Wallingford had nearly tripled output by creating an apple-grading machine (which he then patented) and a controlled-atmosphere storage building. Turning his attention to winter sports, he went on to revolutionize both grooming and snowmaking. Early snowmaking systems (tower guns, the "Otto-matic" fan guns, and air-dried snowmaking systems) and groomers (the "Powder Maker," which dragged a giant spandex steel roller to pulverize snow) sprang from

Otto's fertile imagination. The legacy of these 1960s Auburn inventions is seen not just in Maine but in grooming and snowmaking systems around the world.

Despite its small stature, Lost Valley has spawned an impressive number of skiers that reached the world stage. Karl Anderson, a top-ranked downhiller in the 1970s and the first Mainer on the American Alpine Olympic team, logged serious time on Bull Moose and other Lost Valley trails. Anna, Julie, and Rob Parisien (the "first family" of Maine skiing), who grew up just 3 miles from Lost Valley, all went on to compete in international ski competitions, including the Olympics.

While US Nordic Team member (and Auburn native) John Bower did not learn to ski at Lost Valley, he has his own connections to the mountain. Bower was manager of the resort for the 1965–66 season.

Small as it is, Lost Valley is a hoot to ski. The trails are all well cut, and many follow the fall line from summit to base. Bull Moose, one of the few black diamonds on the hill, doubles as the race slope and makes for a quick shot from top to bottom. Squirrel Run, a green cruiser that skirts the area's northern boundary, provides a leisurely path from the top of Chair #2 to the base lodge. Big Buck and Bobcat, two blues that dump out in front of the lodge, are highly visible trails for skiers that crave an audience. There's also a top-to-bottom park, dubbed Bear Terrain Park, that is accessed from Chair #2.

All slopes at Lost Valley lead to the base lodge, a homey base of operations with a large deck and lovely fireplace. Like many local hills, the base is home to everything visitors need: rentals, food, tickets, and equipment for sale. You can also buy trail tickets to access 15 km of Nordic skiing trails, which are maintained by the Auburn Nordic Skiing Association (www.auburnnordic.org).

To get the full Lost Valley experience, you really have to ski or ride on a weekday afternoon. Around 3 p.m. you'll see bus after bus roll into the parking lot, as hundreds of school ski groups descend on the mountain. Many people learned how to ski (and fell in love with the sport) in an after-school program and these busloads of teen and preteen skiers and snowboarders give me hope for our industry's future. Without affordable community "feeder" slopes like Lost Valley, how would locals learn how to ski?

Given Lost Valley's pedigree, I would not be surprised to see some of their skiers and snowboarders in PyeongChang in 2018.

Location: 200 Lost Valley Rd., Auburn
Contact: (207) 784-1561
Price range: Adults (including seniors) $45, children $40
Number of trails: 14
Difficulty ratings: 6 beginner, 4 intermediate, 4 advanced
Lifts: 1 quad, 3 triples, 1 surface lift
Snowmaking: 98%
Website: http://lostvalleyski.com

MOUNT ABRAM

B ack in the 1950s, brothers Norton, Don, and Stuart Cross were big-time loggers over in western Maine. Among their extensive timber holdings was small but imposing Mount Abram. As they were developing plans to harvest timber on the northeast face, they came up with an idea. The brothers were going to cut harvestable trees anyway, so they cut them in such a way as to open up some ski trails on the side of the mountain.

Thus began a ski area in 1960 that over the next decade was setting the standard for grooming and innovative programs.

With brother Don at the wheel of their Tucker Sno-Cat, their "groom every run every day" policy was, at the time, an innovative concept. Dwarfing their still-nascent neighbor to the north, Sunday River, their experimentation with grooming devices and policies, assisted in great part by their apple-grower friend Otto Wallingford at Lost Valley, another snow farmer of note, led the brothers to be the first to use a "Magic Carpet," a channel iron device with teeth. They also were among Wallingford's first customers for his then-revolutionary "Powder Maker."

With Norton and Don continuing to operate the logging side of the family business, and Stuart and his wife, Jean, running the ski area, their other significant contribution to the industry was their introduction of Maine's first "Learn to Ski Free" program, offering a day of free equipment, lesson, and lift ticket to kids to get them started. That established Mount Abram as the premier learn-to-ski mountain in the state.

However, things were not always rosy for Mount Abram. During a series of tough winters in the 1990s, the mountain was foreclosed on not once, not twice, but three times between 1993 and 2000. Thankfully, things seem to be back on track now. Co-owners Rob Lally and Matt Hancock, who purchased Mount Abram in 2008, have put loads of time, money, and energy into improving the resort as well as its financial affairs. They have also put a huge emphasis on clean energy and sustainability at the area, introducing high-efficiency snowmaking equipment, a biomass boiler to heat the base lodge, free electric-car charging stations, and a solar array that provides the majority of Abram's power.

Five lifts service Abram's 40+ trails, a mix of easy learning slopes, black diamonds, and cruisers. The trails are well cut, and the 650 acres and 1,150 vertical feet make this place feel much more like a mountain. This is aided by the resort's split into two distinct parts: the main mountain above the base lodge serviced by a double chairlift, and the more beginner-friendly slopes on the west side. Nearly all the trails at Abram take their names from the popular Rocky and Bullwinkle cartoon, with names like Rocky's Run and Fearless Leader. However, some trail names are a bit more straightforward, like "The Cliff" on Abram's front face.

Abram's base lodge, constructed in 2012 after a fire destroyed the old one, provides food service along with ticket sales, equipment rentals, and a PSIA ski school. Tickets are $55 for adults, $45 for juniors and seniors, and free if you're over 80 or under 5. There is also a notorious "carload" deal on Friday, when everyone tucked into a car can get tickets for a flat $75.

Location: 308 Howe Hill Rd., Greenwood
Contact: (207) 875-5000
Price range: Adults $55, children and seniors $45
Number of trails: 44
Difficulty ratings: 10 beginner, 21 intermediate, 13 advanced
Lifts: 2 doubles, 1 T-bar, 1 surface, 1 carpet
Snowmaking: 85%
Website: www.mtabram.com

MOUNT JEFFERSON

Byron Delano, with his family, owns and operates this delightful throwback to the days of natural-snow skiing and hospitable, personal friendliness. He was part of a group of Lincoln-area stalwarts who visited Sugarloaf in 1963 and were inspired to throw up a rope tow on a small hill in Lee, about 2 miles from the site of the present ski area. In Byron's words, "We jacked up a tractor, cut grooves in the rear tire, and ran the rope around that." Although it was just for their own enjoyment, skiers from near and far lined up on the road. They not only let them ski, they even set up a hot dog stand to satisfy their visitors' appetites.

That got them to thinking maybe there could be a future for a ski area in town. They looked around the area and there was Mount Jefferson beckoning. They got a local woodsman to cut some trails in exchange for the timber, and then installed a T-bar for the winter of 1964.

Delano bought out his friends in 1980 and has kept the place going, with periodic improvements, since then.

Now the 432-foot mountain boasts two 2,000-foot T-bars, in addition to a handle tow for beginners. Three novice, six intermediate, and three expert trails offer ample variety for both skiers and boarders. Rentals and homemade snacks are available in the base lodge, and tickets are, as one would expect of a family-owned and -focused facility, very reasonably priced.

Adult day tickets are just $20, and a half-day ticket is $15. Youngsters 6 to 12 years of age pay $15 for a full day or $10 for half a day. Kids under 5 ski free, as long as they're accompanied by a paying adult.

If you're planning a visit, be aware that the area only operates Saturday and Sunday, on holidays, and during school vacation weeks.

You can get there by taking SR 6 in Lee, and it's only about an hour northeast of Bangor via the interstate, and just 12 miles east of Lincoln.

Location: SR 6, Lee
Contact: (207) 738-2377
Price range: Adults (including seniors) $20, children $15
Number of trails: 12
Difficulty ratings: 3 beginner, 6 intermediate, 3 advanced
Lifts: 2 T-bars, 1 rope tow
Snowmaking: None
Website: www.skimtjefferson.com

PINNACLE

This local favorite began its life with a rope tow installed on a hill in town in the late 1950s as a project of the Pittsfield Kiwanis Club. A few years later the Pinnacle Ski Club separated from the original founders and took over the operation.

A second rope tow, shorter and with a smaller-diameter rope, was installed on a lower bunny area. Still operated by volunteers, this regional institution has now introduced multiple generations to skiing.

Skiers are asked to become members of the Ski Club at a family rate of $60, couples at $40, and individuals at $20. Rates increase somewhat after December 1 each year. Members are expected to contribute at least 10 hours of service each year.

The club offers free ski and snowboard lessons for all ages. There's night skiing on Friday nights and some selected Saturday nights on the main slope, which is serviced by the 600-foot rope tow.

There are a couple of small side trails and the infamous Headwall, all leading down to the comfy Main Hut with a kitchen where snacks are prepared.

A skating rink and snowboard jumps serve to make this little jewel of a facility the pride of the community.

Location: 271 Waverly St., Pittsfield
Contact: (207) 487-4354
Price range: Adults, children, and seniors annual membership only—$60 per family, $40 per couple, $20 per individual
Number of trails: 8
Difficulty ratings: 2 beginner, 3 intermediate, 3 advanced
Lifts: 2 tow ropes
Snowmaking: None
Website: https://pinnacleskiclub.wordpress.com

POWDER HOUSE HILL

Locals first started skiing on Powder House Hill back in the 1930s, trudging to the top of the 150-foot slope for a few hard-earned runs. Then, shortly after World War II, the Agamenticus Ski Club got a 1938 Ford truck to the top, jacked it up, and installed a rope tow. It was a money-losing operation, so in 1950 the Powder House Ski Club was formed to assume responsibility for its continuing operation and maintenance. And to this day, those responsibilities are still assumed by volunteers at the facility now owned by the town of South Berwick.

As one of only a handful of rope-tow-only ski areas still in existence, Powder House Hill has stayed true to its history of providing ski access for locals and other visitors in southern Maine. When you consider that a lift ticket is just 5 bucks on any of the four days each week the area is open, it qualifies as perhaps the best deal going if you just want to get out and take a few turns on any of the three trails (two novice, one intermediate). The facility has one fan gun to shoot some man-made snow on about 10 percent of the terrain.

The rope tow runs from 7 to 9 p.m. Wednesday and Friday afternoons and evenings (yup, there is even skiing and boarding under the lights!), and noon to 4 p.m. on Saturday and Sunday.

Portland visitors will take exit 19 off the Maine Turnpike to South Berwick and follow Agamenticus Road to the slope. If you are headed north from Portsmouth, take exit 3 to find the area.

Location: Agamenticus Road, South Berwick
Contact: (207) 384-5858
Price range: Adults (including seniors) and children $5 (cash only)
Number of trails: 3
Difficulty ratings: 2 beginner, 1 intermediate
Lifts: 1 rope tow
Snowmaking: None
Website: www.powderhousehill.com

QUOGGY JO

A T-bar serves this 45-acre, 215-vertical-foot mountain about 10 minutes from Presque Isle on SR 167. Owned by the Libra Foundation and operated by the Maine Winter Sports Center, this little gem features two novice trails, three intermediate trails, and a terrain park. Special attention is paid to making this a kid-friendly facility with amenities appealing to the younger set.

Equally appealing is the availability of lift tickets for just $8. Rental ski and snowboard equipment is available on-site.

Overshadowing the small Alpine ski facility are the training headquarters for the US Biathlon Team operated by the Maine Winter Sports Center, where would-be internationally competitive biathletes train in a state-of-the-art environment. It has proven in recent years to be the launch pad for young Mainers to compete and distinguish themselves as world-class competitors.

Location: Fort Fairfield Road, Presque Isle
Contact: (207) 764-3248
Price range: Adults (including seniors) and children $8
Number of trails: 5
Difficulty ratings: 2 beginner, 3 intermediate
Lifts: 1 T-bar
Snowmaking: None
Website: www.skiquoggyjo.org

SADDLEBACK

Whenever we go to Saddleback, we're struck by two simultaneous yet conflicting thoughts. The first is how much it has changed from the mountain many Maine skiers fell in love with in the 1990s. The other is how much it still feels like a step back in time to classic Maine skiing.

There is an argument to be made that Saddleback, more than any other Maine mountain, is in our blood. John Christie owned the resort in the early 1970s, a period that paired his ambitious expansion plans with the crises of gas shortages and terrible winters. Though John had left the mountain a decade before his son Josh (that's me) was born, it was a regular weekend trip during his formative years as a skier. Compared to their regular haunts like the Camden Snow Bowl and Squaw Mountain, Saddleback's steep, narrow trails, glades, and perpetual hoar frost gave the feel of a real "big mountain" experience.

Under the stewardship of the Berry family (who bought the resort in 2003), Saddleback has seen significant improvement to facilities and snowmaking, not to mention an increase in terrain of nearly 50 percent. Among the material changes in the last decade were two new quad chairlifts, a brand-new base lodge, a midmountain "yurt" cafe and warming hut, and increased snowmaking capacity. The beginner's area below the lodge, friendly to families and brand-new skiers, has developed light-years beyond what it used to be.

One of the mountain's marketing lines for the last few years has been "bigger than you think," and it's apt—the mountain of today looms much larger than even the "big" resort of my youth. And yet, despite all these improvements, Saddleback still skis like the resort of two decades ago. The weekend crowds, while larger, never feel as big as at places like Sugarloaf and Sunday River. The base lodge still feels like it has more locals than people from away. The terrain (new and old) is narrow, steep, and loaded with tight corners, and the glades are tightly cut in the old New England tradition. For better or worse, the

Rangeley Chair, a decades-old double chair, feels as slow and creaky (and cold) as always.

The Kennebago Steeps, arguably the biggest change to on-mountain terrain in Saddleback's recent history, splits the difference between old and new just like the rest of the mountain. Made up of expert terrain to the southwest of Saddleback's summit, the Kennebago area was first developed by former owner Donald Breen in the late 1970s (following up, in fact, on some of John's earlier plans to install a lift to reach the mountain's alpine zone). Breen installed a Hall T-bar serving the area in 1979. This T-bar was replaced by the Berrys with a fixed grip quad in 2008.

The new lift, new yurt, new snow guns, and new trails in the Kennebago area—including the 44-acre Casablanca Glade—all fit into the "new" column of Saddleback's identity. Despite the recency of their development, the trails themselves feel like classics. Muleskinner, a favorite of mine (and a bit of a hike from the top of the quad), is worth the effort for a narrow, winding trail with fun drops, small chutes, and several spots to drop into Casablanca. Black Beauty and Frostbite, both on the other side of the massive glade, offer a fairly straight shot over impressive fields of moguls. Tight Line, just like Bronco Buster before it, remains a ski-chatteringly fast, steep groomer. And, of course, there's Casablanca itself, home to some of the best tree skiing in Maine.

While it feels to me like the twelve trails and glades that make up the Kennebago Steeps are old-school northeastern skiing, Saddleback will quickly remind you that is not exactly true. The mix of black and double-black diamonds serviced by a single lift (and without any easier trails mixed in) is in fact unique. It makes it, they claim, the "largest steep skiing and riding facility in the East."

The midmountain of Saddleback is a satisfying mix of beginner and intermediate trails, serviced by two double chairs and a T-bar. Blues like Red Devil, Blue Devil, and Silver Doctor benefit from light traffic and late-day sun, making them a great place to spend the afternoon. Grey Ghost, home to many of the resort's Alpine races, is a fun high-speed cruiser (my pals and I used to use a GPS device to see how fast we could get moving on this one), and Royal Coachman puts exhibitionist skiers and riders on display under the Rangeley Chair. A few terrain parks near the lodge on Wheeler, Montreal, and Gee Whiz round out the mid- and lower-mountain terrain.

The base lodge, rebuilt by the Berrys in 2004, offers a great base of operations: ticket sales, rentals, the ski school, condo rentals, ski patrol, and even the local bar (the Swig 'n' Smelt Pub) are all run out of the single facility. The fact that everything is in one place—and all the trails on the hill lead there—is another piece of Saddleback's culture that feels like an older community hill. And while ticket prices have inched up over the last decade, the resort seems committed to keeping the lifts as inexpensive as possible. If you are willing to plan around weekday promotions or scheduled Maine Days, there are deals to be had.

(It is also worth mentioning that, in an admirable move, Saddleback allows student skiers in grades K–12 who make the honor roll to buy a season pass for $149.)

Often when I'm recommending ski areas to friends and readers, I try to narrow down their choices by asking what they are looking for: a small local hill or one of the big resorts? Budget prices or lots of facilities? Thankfully, Saddleback is a place I can just suggest to everyone.

After a decade of significant improvement, Saddleback's future remains to be seen. The Berry family sold the resort in early 2016. Hopefully, the new owners will continue the much-loved resort's upward trajectory.

Location: 976 Saddleback Mountain Rd., Rangeley
Contact: (207) 864-5671
Price range: Adults $69, children $59, seniors $19
Number of trails: 66
Difficulty ratings: 23 beginner, 20 intermediate, 23 advanced
Lifts: 2 quads, 2 doubles, 1 T-bar
Snowmaking: 85%
Website: www.saddlebackmaine.com

SHAWNEE PEAK

Unassuming Shawnee Peak, located on Mountain Road in Bridgton, looms large in the world of Maine skiing. First opened as Pleasant Mountain in 1938, Shawnee is the longest continually operating ski area in the state. Despite a myriad of changes in ownership (and even a name change) over the last seven decades, Shawnee has survived and thrived while other Maine community hills have disappeared.

The ski area opened in January of 1938 not as Shawnee Peak but as Pleasant Mountain. Pleasant Mountain was first developed by a team of 125 workers, largely funded by a Works Progress Administration grant. While Pleasant wasn't the only ski slope in Maine developed with funding from the WPA (there were also trails cut on Bigelow, Cameron, and Megunticook), it's the only one still in operation today. The mountain was served during that first season by a 1,100-foot rope, which pulled skiers to the top of a single trail—the Wayshego Trail.

In the 1940s and 1950s, Pleasant Mountain flourished. Its proximity to Conway and Portland brought lots of traffic, and the two decades saw many improvements. In the early 1940s, the first ski school in Maine was founded. Pleasant was also home to the state's first T-bar and first chairlift, both installed in the early 1950s. In 1972 Pleasant expanded to open the East Area, 4 miles of intermediate and expert terrain served by a double chairlift and a new second base area.

Eventually, the resort's luck soured. Low snow years in the early 1980s sank the mountain's days of operation, and a 1983 fire destroyed the base lodge. Hundreds of thousands of dollars were invested into snowmaking, but it was too little, too late. The financially strapped owners sold the resort to Pennsylvania's Shawnee Mountain Corporation. Along with changing the name to Shawnee Peak, the new owners added lights for night skiing, improved facilities, and added a new chairlift before running into their own financial issues. Chet Homer, from Tom's (the company of Maine fame), purchased Shawnee in 1994.

There is a lot to love about Shawnee Peak, starting with the unbeatable view. Looking down the lift line of the Summit Express, skiers are treated to a view of Moose Pond, often dotted with ice-fishing huts and snowmobilers. A glance to the west reveals New Hampshire's presidential range and the imposing Mount Washington. Shawnee even shines at night; twenty-some lit trails make the resort the largest night-skiing spot in northern New England.

My favorite way to work Shawnee Peak is east to west. After a quick warm-up on the Headwall and East Slope (a pitchy combo of trails that have been raced on since my dad's day in the 1950s), it is worth moving over to the Sunnyside Triple. The sun hits these trails first, and by midmorning they soften up beautifully. Upper Appalachian, the Gut, and Tycoon are all no-joke expert trails, steep and narrow and worth hitting early. Next come the Dungeons and Cody's Caper, tight glades in the New England tradition. All the summit glades are pretty visible from both of the long chairs. If you plan on skiing the trees, be ready to put on a show.

The middle of the mountain is home to a couple of straightforward, wide-open cruisers, including the original trail from 1938 (now renamed Jack Spratt). The central trails get loads of traffic and it is best to hit them early before they get too skied off, especially if there is not much fresh snow. The trails to the west of the summit are skinny and loaded with turns, and keeping skiers to the left both above and below the midstation is the best way to string together some longer runs.

Shawnee also has a slick terrain park, complete with a "Big Air Bag," a massive inflatable pillow that sits below an 8-foot kicker. Tickets can be purchased for the right to jump onto the inflatable feature at a rate of $12 for two jumps or $15 for four. On Saturday nights the Big Air Bag can be used as a landing pad for snow tubers.

If you are headed up to ski without packing a lunch, Shawnee offers a few culinary options. The main base lodge is home to a cafeteria with the expected ski area spread: soups, sandwiches, and made-to-order food on the grill. There are similar options at the cafeteria in the East Lodge, which is open on weekends and holidays. Blizzard's Pub, located on the upper floor of the lodge, is a homey and traditional ski pub, with burgers, nachos, and local beer on draft. Located less than an hour from Portland and only about 30 minutes from Conway, Shawnee Peak is an easier day trip than other Maine mountains for most skiers. If you do need a place to stay, there are plenty of motels, hotels, and B&Bs in Bridgton and Fryeburg. Shawnee also has some unique lodging options. In addition to on-mountain condos, the mountain just opened the East Lodge Bunkhouse, an apartment above the East Area's base lodge that sleeps twelve people. There is also the Pleasant Mountain Yurt and Cabin, both lift-accessible and located near the mountain's summit.

If you have put off skiing Shawnee in favor of "bigger" mountains, it is time to reconsider. The historic resort has plenty to offer skiers and riders—there is a reason people have been coming here for over seventy-five years.

Location: 119 Mountain Rd., Bridgton
Contact: (207) 647-8444
Price range: Adults $55, children and seniors $45
Number of trails: 44
Difficulty ratings: 7 beginner, 23 intermediate, 14 advanced
Lifts: 1 quad, 2 triples, 1 double, 1 carpet
Snowmaking: 98%
Website: www.shawneepeak.com

SPRUCE MOUNTAIN

Tiny Spruce Mountain is among Maine's longest-lived ski areas, dating back as far as the Eisenhower administration. The Spruce Mountain Ski Club started in 1956, looking to develop a ski area in North Jay, Maine. Though Spruce initially opened with a rope tow near North Jay's Spruce Mountain Road in '56, the whole enterprise moved to a more accessible location in Livermore Falls just a few years later.

Spruce was small when it opened with that single rope tow in the 1950s, and it stayed small in the following decades. Currently, the area (now owned jointly by the towns of Jay, Livermore Falls, and Livermore) hosts eleven trails on 300 vertical feet, serviced by three rope tows. The rope tows are truly a relic of the earlier days of Maine skiing. In fact, Spruce *insists* newcomers use work gloves or leather gloves while using the tow so they don't ruin their regular ski gloves.

Spruce is a family-friendly and beginner-friendly hill, with lots of great learning slopes that all lead to the small base area. Among the 11 trails, the two black diamonds—Face and Bowl—offer a quick thrill but little challenge to advanced skiers.

The hill boasts 50 percent snowmaking coverage, and a single Pisten Bully groomer maintains the slopes. Rather than operating all week during ski season, Spruce is open on Wednesday and Friday nights and all day on Saturday and Sunday. Lift tickets are a steal compared to many larger resorts, at $25 for a full day and during vacation weeks and only $18 for nights.

Spruce is run by a mostly volunteer force of locals. Volunteers are incentivized by a refund program that credits $50 toward a season pass for 8 hours of volunteer work.

The small resort offers lessons for a variety of ages and ski levels, and a comfortable base lodge sits at the base of the easy Barn slope. The menu at the lodge's food court offers, bar none, the best value in the state of Maine. The whole Spruce menu (priced between $1 and $3) is a steal, but the famous $1 grilled cheese has gained well-deserved legendary status. While there are no rentals or lodging available at Spruce, nearby Wilton, Jay, and Farmington have plenty of options.

Spruce Mountain is also home to 5 km of Nordic ski trails, which can also be used for snowshoeing.

Location: Ski Slope Road, Jay
Contact: (207) 879-4090
Price range: Adults $25, children $20, seniors 65+ free
Number of trails: 11
Difficulty ratings: 3 beginner, 5 intermediate, 3 advanced
Lifts: 3 rope tows
Snowmaking: 50%
Website: www.sprucemountain.org

SUGARLOAF

Sugarloaf looms large in the world of eastern skiers, and with good reason. The Carrabassett Valley resort is not just the largest ski resort in Maine (though it is, by a long shot)—it is the largest ski area east of the Mississippi River. The first trail at Sugarloaf was cut in the 1950s, and by the mid-1960s the mountain was already a player on the national stage. In the following decade the story of Sugarloaf has only grown, with recent expansions pushing the resort far beyond its original boundaries to the peak of neighboring Burnt Mountain.

Sugarloaf's story started back in the summer of 1950, when a group of Kingfield residents cut a trail on Sugarloaf. Led by Amos Winter, these "Bigelow Boys" cut Winter's Way (which opened in the winter of 1951), soon followed by trails like Narrow Gauge, Sluice, Tote Road, and Double Bitter. The first surface lifts were installed soon after, but it was the installation of the Sugarloaf Gondola in 1965 that really put Sugarloaf on the world stage. The lift spanned from Sugarloaf's base to summit, over 8,000 feet of lift that deposited skiers in Sugarloaf's above-tree-line snowfields. The expansion, along with a conscious rebranding of Sugarloaf to Sugarloaf USA, led to hugely successful years for the resort.

Throughout the '70s and '80s, the installation of a number of chairlifts (as well as the construction of a "village" area around Sugarloaf's base lodge) further grew the ski area. The '90s saw the installation of the Superquad, Sugarloaf's first high-speed detachable quad, and the Timberline quad to Sugarloaf's summit, along with new trails cut underneath these lifts. Soon after being purchased by Boyne Resorts in 2007 (along with sister resort Sunday River), Sugarloaf announced an ambitious plan for expansion and improvement called Sugarloaf 2020. Along with new lifts and village improvements, the plan expands Sugarloaf to the east, swallowing up much of neighboring Burnt Mountain.

(One of the authors of this guide also wrote the definitive history of Sugarloaf, which looks at the resort's past with much greater detail. If you're interested in delving deeper into the ski area's history, grab a copy of John Christie's *The Story of Sugarloaf*.)

All the statistics around Sugarloaf—terrain, vertical, acreage, and the like—are characterized by the word "most." Skiable vertical feet? 2,820, the most in New England. Acreage? 1,230 developed, skiable acres, the most east of the Rocky Mountains. Trails? 161, the most in Maine. On top of this, Sugarloaf's summit is at 4,237 feet, only topped in Maine by the massive Mount Katahdin.

For expert skiers, the terrain on Sugarloaf's east side is some of the most technical, challenging, and downright fun trails on the mountain. Starting around Winter's Way, Sugarloaf's first trail, cut by hand in 1950 and extending all the way to the summit of Burnt Mountain, you find a mix of trails made mostly of single and double black diamonds. Most of Sugarloaf's glades and ungroomed, natural "wild thing" trails sit on this side of the mountain.

Stretching into the woods beyond bumpy Ripsaw in the King Pine area, easternmost terrain is made up of three fairly distinct areas: the Cant Dog glades and Brackett Basin, the Eastern Territory, and Burnt Mountain.

Cant Dog, which was first cut about a decade ago, has expanded into a number of hand-cut chutes and glades that dump skiers back at the King Pine lift. Brackett Basin, just beyond this, features a mix of tight glades, more wide-open areas, and cliffs on trails like Birler and Sweeper that eventually funnel skiers down to King Pine or Whiffletree.

A traverse on the Golden Road trail, which necessitates a lot of skating or removing your equipment to hike, leads to the commercially logged Eastern Territory. The terrain features spectacular wide-open glades that funnel skiers past Sugarloaf's base area and onto a mix of Nordic and hiking trails. It takes some effort, but eventually riders work their way back to Snubber, almost 400 vertical feet below the base lodge.

The King Pine Bowl itself, serviced by a fixed-grip quad and the Skyline lift, is a playground of steep, expert terrain. Widowmaker offers a perfect consistent pitch that rolls onto the heart-in-your-throat steep Flume. Misery Whip, the former home of the #5 T-bar, is a narrow can't-miss-a-turn shot that is only about a groomer track wide. Even Haul Back, a trail that seems to occasionally fight with the natural fall line, is fun to ski. Its home under the chairlift makes it perfect for exposition.

Between King Pine and Winter's Way is a handful of steep, straight adrenaline shots. Accessible from the summit or the Spillway crosscut, trails like Gondola Line and White Nitro, the steepest trail in the East, simply drop away from under you.

Whiffletree, the kid- and beginner-friendly area below the King Pine Bowl, also offers unique thrills. Poleline, a beginner-to-intermediate trail below Boomauger, offers fun rolls down a slope dotted with utility poles. Buckboard is a narrow, twisting cruiser in the classic New England mold and affords stunning views of the Bigelow range. Even the newly revamped Moose Alley is a hoot, recalling a luge run of banked turns, though a new sign warns that adults aren't allowed in without children.

The center of the mountain, from Winter's Way to Tote Road, boasts the "longest continuous fall line in New England," with famous trails like the FIS-approved Narrow Gauge, Competition Hill, Hayburner, and Sugarloaf's signature bump run, Skidder. The West Mountain shines in the afternoon, where the sun shines until late in the day on blue and green cruisers. Below all this (and, in fact, below Sugarloaf's base lodge), the Birches and Landing beginner areas offer flat terrain for first-timers.

It is all capped by Sugarloaf's legendary Snowfields, the above-tree-line skiing on Sugarloaf's summit that inspired the resort's iconic logo. The snowfields and backside of the mountain (accessible by a short hike from the top of the Timberline quad) provide a panoramic view of Vermont, New Hampshire, Canada, and Mount Katahdin. Snow and powder last for days in the snowfields, and the lack of any trees or shrubs leaves skiers to design their own route home.

Rather than a menagerie of base areas and lodges, all of Sugarloaf dumps back to a single, central base lodge and village. Rentals, lessons, and ticket sales are available in the lodge, while neighboring buildings hold restaurants (go to the Bag and Kettle for their famous Bag Burger and house-made beer) and retail shops. Just behind the lodge are on-hill rooms at the Sugarloaf Inn and Sugarloaf Mountain Hotel, the latter of which just installed a thirty-person hot tub under the chairlift. There is further lodging available on the mountain in the form of rental condominiums. Options for rooms on the drive up SR 27 have thinned over the last decade, but larger towns nearby (Farmington in particular) have plenty of options if you do not mind a bit of a drive.

Like its sister resort Sunday River, Sugarloaf has the distinction of some of Maine's most expensive lift tickets: $86 a day for adults, $70 for teens (13 to 18), and $60 for juniors and seniors (under 13 and over 65, respectively). There are a couple of options for skiers looking to save money, including discounts when tickets are pre-purchased at sugarloaf.com and a Frequent Skier Card that buys discounted tickets all season long.

Location: 5092 Access Rd., Carrabassett Valley
Contact: (207) 237-2000
Price range: Adults $86, children $70, seniors $60
Number of trails: 146
Difficulty ratings: 34 beginner, 49 intermediate, 63 advanced
Lifts: 2 high-speed quads, 3 quads, 1 triple, 6 doubles, 1 T-bar, 2 surface lifts
Snowmaking: 95%
Website: www.sugarloaf.com

The lodge and main slopes at the Baker Mountain Ski Tow Club. BAKER

Looking up Big Squaw from the base lodge. In the background, some of Big Squaw's older trails are visible. PHOTO BY AUTHOR (JOHN CHRISTIE)

The newly renovated base lodge at Big Squaw. PHOTO BY AUTHOR (JOHN CHRISTIE)

Author John Christie, skiing corduroy near the Camden Snow Bowl summit.
DAVID RIDLEY

The Camden Snow Bowl is the only eastern ski resort where you can see the Atlantic Ocean from the slopes. CAMDEN SNOW BOWL

A view of the trails and rope tow (Tow 2) at Eaton Mountain. DAVID S. BEERS, EATON MOUNTAIN

Fresh snow and Eastern powder at Shawnee Peak. SHAWNEE PEAK

Looking across Moose Pond at the slopes of Shawnee Peak. SHAWNEE PEAK

Fireworks light up the night sky during Shawnee Peak's annual Winterfest celebration.
SHAWNEE PEAK

Carving spring corn at Sugarloaf. SUGARLOAF

Cross country trails wind around the base of Sugarloaf in Carrabassett Valley. SUGARLOAF

Cross country skiers glide across the trails, with Sugarloaf towering in the background.
SUGARLOAF

Looking up "The Main," the main slope at Titcomb Mountain. MEGAN ROBERTS, TITCOMB MOUNTAIN

A young skier attacks one of the well-cut glades at Titcomb Mountain. MEGAN ROBERTS, TITCOMB MOUNTAIN

A look back at the slopes of Titcomb Mountain in 1942, its first year in operation.
TITCOMB MOUNTAIN

A skier pulling her child in a pulk sled enjoying the beautiful sunshine in Carter's Cross Country Ski Center pasture trail. CARTER'S CROSS COUNTRY CENTER

Dave Carter testing out his 12-foot wooden skis at Carter's Cross Country Ski Center.
CARTER'S CROSS COUNTRY CENTER

The Nordic practice of skijoring is alive and well in Fort Kent. FORT KENT OUTDOOR CENTER

Nordic racers depart at the Fort Kent Outdoor Center. FORT KENT OUTDOOR CENTER

The 10th Mountain Lodge at the Fort Kent Outdoor Center. FORT KENT OUTDOOR CENTER

World Cup racers take off at the Nordic Heritage Center in Aroostook County.
NORDIC HERITAGE CENTER

Flagstaff Lake, one of the huts on the Maine Huts and Trails network. MAINE HUTS AND TRAILS

A fire roars in front of one of the on-hill cabins available to rent at Shawnee Peak.
SHAWNEE PEAK

Little Lyford Lodge, one of the huts in the Appalachian Mountain Club's Maine Wilderness Lodges network. MAINE WILDERNESS LODGES

SUNDAY RIVER

In the world of Maine ski areas, Newry's Sunday River is one of the state's few destination resorts. Along with its sister resort, Sugarloaf, Sunday River draws people from states (and even nations) away and plays host to multiple hotels, restaurants, and other facilities. With 135 trails spread across 870 acres on eight distinct peaks, Sunday River offers an experience that is not far removed from the large resorts of the western United States or Europe. The amazing realization is that this resort did not always look like Sunday River's destiny. Decades ago it seemed Sunday River might stay a midsize community slope.

Sunday River first opened as Sunday River Skiway in the final days of the 1950s, served by a single surface lift on Bald Mountain. Throughout the '60s and '70s, the area expanded modestly, building surface lifts on what would become the Locke and Barker Mountain areas. The big change came in the 1980s when Les Otten purchased Sunday River. Otten grew the resort exponentially, adding six new distinct mountain areas in the next decade: North Peak ('85), Spruce Peak ('86), Whitecap ('87), Aurora Peak ('91), Jordon Bowl ('94), and Oz ('95). Suddenly, Sunday River was a premier resort.

After a decade managed by American Skiing Company, Sunday River (along with Sugarloaf) was purchased by Boyne USA Resorts in 2007. In the years since, Sunday River has seen consistent but measured improvement to its facilities and terrain, including the installation of a combined chairlift/gondola (or "chondola") to North Peak.

It is worth noting that this is but a brief overview of Sunday River's fascinating history. In fact, it is one of the few resorts in Maine that has warranted its own book. For a richer look at the Newry resort's past, check out Dave Irons's excellent history *Sunday River: Honoring the Past, Embracing the Future*, published in 2009.

Today, Sunday River sprawls across eight distinct peaks, each with a slightly different personality. Given the mountain's northern exposure, it makes the most sense for skiers to start their day on the eastern peaks and work west with the sun. White Cap, the easternmost area, offers some of Sunday River's most challenging terrain. It is a mix of steeps, bumps, and trees, and home of "White Heat," which for years was advertised as the longest, widest, steepest trail in the East. Next is Locke Mountain, the home of Sunday River's original trails and still the most traditional East Coast trails (read: narrow, winding) at the resort. Barker Mountain is the guts of the resort, offering access to peaks to the east or west from its summit. It's also usually the first part of the resort to open in the fall and the last to close in the spring. Spruce's eight trails are largely groomed cruisers, and neighboring North Peak hosts Sunday River's massive, award-winning terrain parks. Tucked behind Spruce Peak, Aurora mixes tight glades with steeps, including Sunday River's steepest pitch on Black Hole. Oz is dominated by natural and ungroomed snow and terrain, making it an experts-only playground that plays to skiers who prefer side- or backcountry to maintained slopes. Finally there's Jordon Bowl, on Sunday River's westernmost boundary, home to wide-open cruisers and breathtaking views of Mount Washington and the Presidential Range.

Sunday River's spread-out design means that the resort has a number of different lodges where visitors can start their day. The bases of White Cap and Barker both feature day lodges with food courts and other dining options, along with lift ticket sales and small retail shops. The larger South Ridge Lodge is the main hub of the resort and hosts those amenities along with a larger ski shop, equipment rentals, lessons, and even a real estate office. The eastern and western ends of the resort also offer on-hill lodging (and attached dining), with the Grand Summit Hotel and Jordan Grand, respectively.

Along with size comes price, and Sunday River's lift tickets are the most expensive in Maine: $89 a day for adults, $69 for teens, and $59 for juniors and seniors. Like their sister resort, Sugarloaf, Sunday River offers a few ways to save, including discounts when tickets are pre-purchased at sundayriver.com and a Frequent Skier Card that buys season-long discounted tickets. There is also at least one guaranteed option for free skiing at Sunday River: On the final day of each season (usually the first weekend in May), the resort offers lift tickets to all visitors free of cost.

Location: 15 South Ridge Rd., Newry
Contact: (800) 543-2754
Price range: Adults $89, children $69, seniors $59
Number of trails: 129
Difficulty ratings: 32 beginner, 52 intermediate, 45 advanced
Lifts: 1 chondola, 4 high-speed quads, 5 quads, 3 triples, 1 double, 1 surface
Snowmaking: 96%
Website: www.sundayriver.com

TITCOMB MOUNTAIN

Generations of recreational and competitive skiers have made their first turns on this gem of a nonprofit, locally supported area, located just west of downtown Farmington. This mountain is on the route up to Sugarloaf and Saddleback, each less than an hour to the northwest, and both ski areas benefit greatly from this incubator for lifelong winter sports enthusiasts.

It was back in 1940 that a Model T Ford–powered rope tow dragged its first initiates up to the top of a slope that had been cleared by the Franklin Ski and Outing Club. World War II interrupted the continuing operation of the area, as it did for many areas in the state. But after the end of hostilities, locals reopened the area and began a program of continuing improvement.

Skiers in the 1950s benefited from the installation of a Poma lift on which budding competitors rode up to train on slalom courses set on the steep grade above the base lodge. In 1956 *Down East* magazine wrote, "The physical layout of Titcomb's operation is impressive enough, but the Club's greatest achievement is the almost professional system into developing young skiers into topflight competitors."

The addition of a cross-country trail network (now totaling some 16 km) and the erection of a wooden trestle jump turned the area into a venue for four-event competitions of the highest level.

Today, skiers and boarders put on their gear in a cozy base lodge with a snack bar and ascend the 750-foot slope and trail network on either of the two T-bars, while beginners cut their teeth on a handle lift. There is also a terrain park for budding and proficient boarders.

Four novice, five intermediate, and six expert trails offer assuredly good conditions thanks to snowmaking coverage on about 75 percent of the terrain. Thanks to an extensive lighting system, the area is open from 3 to 6 p.m. on Monday, Tuesday, and Thursday; 3 to 8 p.m. on Wednesday; and until 8 p.m. on Saturday when conditions allow. Weekend and holiday hours are 9 a.m. to 4 p.m.

True to its mission, the area has kept rates very low, so anyone can ski on the weekend for just $22 a day on the T-bars and $5 on the pony lift. Evening rates are just $10 for college kids, young adults, and juniors and $15 for adults. The fee for access to the Nordic trails is $10 as well.

Groups of ten or more can ski all day on weekends at the half-day rate of just $15.

There are many places to pick from for lodging and dining in Farmington, home to one of the campuses of the University of Maine system.

Location: 180 Ski Slope Rd., West Farmington
Contact: (207) 778-9031
Price range: Adults (including seniors) and children $22
Number of trails: 15
Difficulty ratings: 4 beginner, 5 intermediate, 6 advanced
Lifts: 2 T-bars, 1 handle tow
Snowmaking: 75%
Website: www.titcombmountain.com

Nordic (cross-country) Areas

BETHEL NORDIC SKI CENTER

Bethel is thought by many to be the cross-country ski capital of Maine, and with good reason. The 35 km of classic and skate groomed trails of the center, starting right in the middle of the village, offer mountain vistas and gentle terrain. The forested segments include challenges for skiers of all abilities and invite visitors to take excursions of any length.

Meticulous grooming adds to the appeal. For those who prefer trekking out on snowshoes, there are 5 miles of snowshoeing trails as well.

There is an on-premise shop where you can purchase lessons and gear rental is available. The shop also offers additional gear for purchase, including wax, socks, mittens, and gloves.

Feel free to bring along your canine companion, as there is a 1.5 km dog-friendly loop.

There is a $20 fee for all-day use of the trails, and after 1 p.m. it drops to $16. Students and skiers over 63 years of age pay just $16 for the entire day.

Location: Bethel
Contact: (207) 824-6276
Price range: Adults $20, children and seniors $16
Trails: 35 km
Available amenities: Rentals, warming hut
Snowshoeing allowed? Yes
Website: www.caribourecreation.com

BLACK MOUNTAIN

For nearly half a century, Black Mountain in Rumford has been recognized as one of the very best Nordic skiing facilities, for both recreational skiers and competitors, in North America. The cross-country network was developed by Maine Ski Hall of Famer and two-time Olympian Chummy Broomhall. He designed not only the trail system at his native Black Mountain, but his skills were called upon to lay out the Olympic trails at both Lake Placid and Squaw Valley.

His technical skills were also further proved in the development of revolutionary trail-grooming equipment.

The Black Mountain facility hosted US Cross Country Championships in 2003, 2004, and 2011 So when you cruise the trails, you will be doing so in the tracks of famous Olympians who have skied the same layout.

Seventeen km of trails groomed for both classic and skate skiing originate at the comfortable lodge located at the base of the area's Alpine facilities. Some 4 km also boast man-made snow to assure quality conditions even when Mother Nature fails to cooperate.

Fifteen dollars a day gives the visitor access to the entire network, and children under 5 and people over 75 ski for free.

Location: Rumford
Contact: (207) 364-8977
Price range: $15, children under 5 and seniors over 75 free
Trails: 17 km
Available amenities: Warming hut
Snowshoeing allowed? Yes
Website: http://skiblackmountain.org

CARTER'S CROSS COUNTRY SKI CENTER

Helping solidify the Bethel area's reputation as a Nordic mecca, Carter's two facilities, one off the Intervale Road in Bethel and the other on SR 26 in Oxford, offer unmatched terrain and variety for cross-country skiers of every taste and ability.

Each area has a warming hut, and the retail shop features the best in equipment and gear, along with a complete rental touring outfit for just $15 if you are looking to test out both your ability and the most up-to-date gear. For kids under 4 feet tall, the whole outfit is just $10.

The Bethel network is made up of thirteen trails, and the Oxford layout has nineteen trails. The former is open daily from 9 a.m. to 4 p.m., the latter 10 a.m. to 5 p.m.

Tickets are $15 for adults and $10 for youths 6 to 18 years old and seniors. Children under 6 can ski for free.

There is a dog-friendly trail as well, but you are asked to call ahead before you plan to arrive. The charge to use that trail is $14.

Location: Bethel and Oxford
Contact: (207) 824-3880 (Bethel), (207) 539-4848 (Oxford)
Price range: Adults $15, children and seniors $10, children under 6 free
Trails: 55 km (Bethel), 30 km (Oxford)
Available amenities: Rentals, warming hut
Snowshoeing allowed? Yes
Website: http://cartersxcski.com

FIVE FIELDS FARM

Located just 5 miles south of Bridgton on SR 107, you will spot both the warming hut and the farm stand that mark the start of a trail system that totals 27 km of cross-country pleasure. The trails loop around orchards and connect with logging roads and with land owned by abutting property owners, including the Loon Echo Land Trust on picturesque Bald Pate Mountain.

Although the trails are not groomed all the way to the summit of Bald Pate, more accomplished and adventurous skiers often take the 20-minute trek to the top, if for no other reason than to take in the view that includes numerous lakes and ponds and, on a clear day, glistening Mount Washington to the west.

As a bonus to skiers that bring along four-legged friends, Five Fields Farm is dog-friendly. Beginning skiers will find the entire network to be inviting and negotiable, and rental equipment is available in all sizes.

Five Fields is open daily from 9 a.m. until dusk; $12 trail pass, $16 rental equipment.

Location: Bridgton
Contact: (207) 647-2869
Price range: Adults (including seniors) and children $12
Trails: 27 km
Available amenities: Warming hut, rentals
Snowshoeing allowed? Yes
Website: http://fivefieldsski.com

FORT KENT OUTDOOR CENTER

Way up in the northernmost tip of the state, and farther to the north of Bangor, there is a state-of-the-art training and competition facility. This facility hosts not only local potential biathlon competitors but also the best in the world for national and World Cup meets. This venue has received universal kudos from the biathlon community.

The center, underwritten by the Libra Foundation and developed and operated by the Maine Winter Sports Center, provides both training facilities for competitors and superbly maintained trails for recreational cross-country skiing.

For dedicated competitors there is a lighted roller ski loop, and 23 km of skiing trails invite skiers of all abilities.

A 5,500-square-foot lodge anchors the complex, and a waxing facility with twenty-six rooms provides fine-tuning space for serious competitors.

Trail use and equipment are free for children 6 and under. Open daily, conditions permitting.

Location: Fort Kent
Contact: (207) 834-6203
Price range: Adults (including seniors) $14, children $10
Trails: 23 km
Available amenities: Warming hut, rentals
Snowshoeing allowed? Yes
Website: http://10thmtskiclub.org

HARRIS FARM XC
CENTER

To prove that there is superior cross-country skiing all over the state, this southern Maine treasure offers 40 km of diversified touring fun across open fields and through sheltered stands of trees. All this is thanks to the Harris family, who delight in sharing their 500-acre dairy and vegetable farm with eager winter-sports enthusiasts. You will find it on Buzzell Hill Road a few miles west of Biddeford.

The comfortable and inviting lodge features a large common room, where folks can gather around a crackling woodstove, and includes restrooms and a kitchen area.

On weekends you can buy hot dogs, snacks, and hot drinks, or you are invited to bring your own lunch to enjoy in the large sunroom. Be sure to sample some of Harris Farm's delicious chocolate milk for a special treat.

There is a fully stocked retail and rental shop, where you can even try out a pair of snowshoes. There are also rental sleds available for your little ones to try out on the small, safe hill right in clear view in front of the lodge.

Skis, boots, and poles are available to rent for $15 a day for adults and $10 for kids 12 and under. Snowshoe rentals are $10, and a sled will cost you $5 an hour.

If you are thinking of taking up cross-country skiing for the first time and have your own equipment, 1-hour group lessons (by appointment only) are available for $18, or a private lesson will cost you $30. There is a complete Learn to Ski package for $40, which includes rental equipment, a lesson, and trail access. This is also by appointment only.

Adults can access the trails on weekends for $15 and midweek for just $12. Students ages 7 to 18 pay $10 on Saturday and Sunday and

$8 during the week. Full-time college students and seniors over 65 can ski Monday through Friday for just $10. During nonholiday weeks dogs are welcome in the ski area.

Location: Dayton
Contact: (207) 499-2678
Price range: Adults $15, children and seniors $10
Trails: 40 km
Available amenities: Warming hut, rentals
Snowshoeing allowed? Yes
Website: http://harrisfarm.com

HIDDEN VALLEY
NATURE CENTER

Encompassing about 1,000 acres of unspoiled Lincoln County woodland off Egypt Road in Jefferson, this unique community-based and -supported nonprofit resource includes 24 km of cross-country trails through the woods and along nearly a mile of Little Dyer Pond shore frontage.

This gem comprises about 10 percent of a much larger, undeveloped region within easy distance of a substantial portion of Maine's population, as identified by the Sheepscot Valley Conservation Association.

The trails lacing through the property are lightly groomed to provide the best possible conditions up and down gently rolling hills, up to rocky outcroppings with beautiful views, and down to the pond's shoreline.

You are apt to encounter folks on snowshoes who are also welcome on the trails and in the comfortable warming hut.

As the nature center is a member-supported enterprise, most trail users opt for the annual family membership of $75, with many taking advantage of the $1,000 lifetime option. Membership eliminates the customary $5 per day use fee charged to other visitors.

Location: Jefferson
Contact: (207) 200-8840
Price range: Adults (including seniors) and children $5
Trails: 24 km
Available amenities: Warming hut
Snowshoeing allowed? Yes
Website: www.hvnc.org

LOST VALLEY TOURING CENTER

From the base of the Lost Valley ski area, visitors can access over 17 km of cross-country ski trails that cover not just the ski resort but also the surrounding fields and woods. The trail network is managed by a unique partnership between the Lost Valley resort and the Auburn Nordic Ski Association (ANSA); Lost Valley provides the land and business backbone for the network, but the trails are groomed and maintained by ANSA members.

The majority of the eleven trails that make up the network sit to the north of the Alpine ski area, filling the forest between Young's Corner Road and Perkins Ridge Road. The exceptions are the intermediate Pond Loop and expert Amos's Path, which run alongside the orchards at the summit of Lost Valley.

Two of the trails in the network, Water's Edge (a pleasant green circle that is cut parallel to Lapham Brook) and the aforementioned Amos's Path, are reserved for classic cross-country "striding." The other nine trails are groomed with both a skating lane and a classic track. The whole network is crisscrossed by snowshoe trails, which are also maintained by ANSA.

Trail access passes at Lost Valley run $10 a day throughout the season. Equipment package rentals are also available at a price of $18 a day.

Trail passes and rentals are available at the Lost Valley base lodge, as are refreshments and other amenities. Lodging is not available at Lost Valley, but there are more than enough lodging options in Auburn.

Location: Auburn
Contact: (207) 784-1561
Price range: Adults (including seniors) and children $10
Trails: 10 km
Available amenities: Warming hut
Snowshoeing allowed? No (but allowed on nearby ANSA trails)
Website: www.lostvalleyski.com

MAINE HUTS
AND TRAILS

When Larry Warren was running the show at Sugarloaf during the boom-to-bust period of the 1970s and 1980s, the seeds for a very different outdoor recreation business model were germinating in his fertile and imaginative mind.

As a firsthand witness to and active participant in the capital-intensive, weather-dependent, and fiscally questionable expansion of ski areas, Warren had a vision for a very different kind of development. He envisioned a ski area that would capitalize on the same stunning virtues of the Maine mountains that make Alpine skiing attractive to so many, but would be a lower-density, less expensive way for people to get out and enjoy the woods.

When he left his position at Sugarloaf in 1986, he devoted his energies to creating what is now Maine's premier network of interconnected huts along a wilderness corridor that parallels a portion of the Appalachian Trail (also known as the "AT") in the western mountains, but avoids the high peaks that mark one of the AT's most difficult sections between Georgia and Mount Katahdin.

Today, his Maine Huts and Trails is a year-round resource for nonmotorized recreation in both summer and winter. These facilities support a growing population of outdoor enthusiasts who are prepared to eschew the convenience (some say clamor) of intensely developed facilities and enjoy nature as many say it should be: quietly, casually, and under one's own power, whether on cross-country skis and snowshoes in the winter or hiking in the summer. All of this in a setting that many of us think is unparalleled in its natural beauty and grandeur.

If you have been on any section of the 50-mile trail or stayed and eaten at any of the four "huts" (actually stunning eco-lodges strategically located at about 12-mile intervals), you are well aware of the unique experience that awaits visitors to this Maine asset.

Each of the huts offers spectacular wilderness vistas while serving as a base for snowshoeing, cross-country skiing, or just relaxing in the arms of nature. In addition, each hut features such unexpected amenities as home-cooked meals with local organic ingredients, comfortable beds, bathrooms with hot showers, and even shuttles to transport your gear from hut to hut.

By allowing inexpensive public access to some of the state's most attractive forest lands, the system is intended to demonstrate environmentally sensitive economic development true to a conservation ethic that can not only fill a need and succeed, but can also provide the opportunity for environmental and experiential education.

Location: Carrabassett Valley
Contact: (207) 265-2400
Price range: Free trail access for adults, children, and seniors
Trails: 72 km
Available amenities: Warming hut
Snowshoeing allowed? Yes
Website: www.mainehuts.org

MAINE WILDERNESS LODGES

Owned and operated by the Appalachian Mountain Club (also known as the AMC), the Maine Wilderness Lodges offer Nordic skiers a chance to explore over 66,000 acres of conservation land that the AMC owns. The Gorman Chairback Lodge and Little Lyford Lodge, nestled in Maine's 100-mile wilderness, mix blissful solitude, amazing terrain, and comfortable amenities for those willing to make the trip. The lodges, east of Moosehead Lake and south of Baxter, show off a part of Maine many tourists (and even locals) never explore.

The trail network is massive, with 80 miles of groomed trails of varying difficulty. The shortest ski-in trip is from a winter parking area to Little Lyford, about 6 miles. Once you are on the network, you can string together inter-lodge and day trips that span dozens of miles.

The lodge-to-lodge ski trail offers groomed backcountry skiing between the Gorman Chairback and Little Lyford lodges, as well as lodges owned by partner West Branch Pond Camps. All three provide meals, hot showers, and a choice between private cabins or a shared bunkhouse space. The AMC even provides a shuttle between cabins, allowing skiers to travel light from place to place.

The lodges have also worked closely with local snowmobile clubs to maintain motorized access, but they keep the snow machines largely away from the ski trails. The result is pleasant skiing and snowshoeing rarely interrupted by the buzz of engines.

The AMC lodges are open to skiers for the bulk of winter, depending on trail conditions; a typical season runs from December through March. They open back up after mud season for summer visitors. Rates at either of the lodges for nonmembers start around $100 for the shared bunkhouses and $150 to $200 for private cabins.

Location: Moosehead Lake
Contact: (603) 466-2727
Price range: Free trail access for adults, children, and seniors
Trails: 100 km
Available amenities: Warming hut
Snowshoeing allowed? Yes
Website: www.outdoors.org

NEW ENGLAND OUTDOOR CENTER

In the southerly shadows of legendary Mount Katahdin, this forested network of groomed cross-country trails can be found just a short distance from the south entrance to Baxter State Park. There are nearly 20 km of trails at the New England Outdoor Center (NEOC), and half hold the distinction of being designed by Olympian John Morton.

The special allure of this winter wonderland lies in the on-site accommodations and cuisine.

Twin Pines Cabins provide comfortable housing, and the River Drivers Restaurant serves up hearty fare to satisfy skiers' hungry appetites. The cabins are available in a variety of sizes and styles, from log cabins with bunk beds to larger guesthouses for families and groups. All of the lodgings have fully equipped kitchens and baths, and the views of Katahdin out over Millinocket Lake are spectacular.

Location: Millinocket
Contact: (207) 723-5438
Price range: Free trail access for adults, children, and seniors
Trails: 20 km
Available amenities: Warming hut
Snowshoeing allowed? Yes
Website: www.neoc.com

NORDIC HERITAGE CENTER

L ocated in Presque Isle, this world-class biathlon competition center has some 20 km of superbly groomed cross-country trails available *completely free of charge*! Some trails are even lit for nighttime skiing from 4:30 to 8:30 p.m.

This is possible thanks to the unique partnership between the center, the Maine Winter Sports Center, City of Presque Isle Recreation, the Aroostook Medical Center, City of Fort Fairfield Recreation, and the University of Maine at Presque Isle dedicated to providing and promoting healthy recreation for youths and adults.

A 6,500-square-foot lodge, open daily from 6 a.m. to 10 p.m., has all the amenities one would expect, including dining.

Adults can rent skis, boots, and poles for $10, with the option to rent just one of those items for only $5. The complete rental package for children is just $7.

When out on the trails, you can delight in following the tracks of the world's best biathletes, as the center has hosted such competitions as the 2006 Biathlon World Junior Championships.

Location: Presque Isle
Contact: (207) 762-6972
Price range: Free trail access for adults, children, and seniors
Trails: 20 km
Available amenities: Rentals, warming hut
Snowshoeing allowed? Yes
Website: http://nordicheritagecenter.org

PINELAND FARMS

L ong before downhill skis and snowboards were favorite tools for winter recreation, their forebears—snowshoes and Nordic skis— were used for transportation. These early implements have shed most of their practical utility because of cars and snowmobiles, but they have been adopted by those hoping to explore the outdoors. One of the best places to experience these sports, whether you are a first-timer or a veteran enthusiast, is New Gloucester's Pineland Farms.

Pineland, a 5,000-acre working farm that is also home to a business campus and loads of recreational opportunities, has evolved greatly from its original purpose. Established in 1908 as the "Maine School for the Feeble Minded," the facility served as a campus for those with mental illness. The school, cobbled together from six local farms, continued to function as a working farm while home to the institution. At its peak the school was considered a national model and housed 1,500 patients.

The facility closed in the mid-1990s and fell into disrepair. The Libra Foundation, one of the largest charitable organizations in Maine (and a supporter of Nordic ski development from Presque Isle to Rumford), purchased the property in 2000 and took to renovating. Now a mix of businesses and organizations occupy the campus composed of nineteen buildings. A 25 km trail system is also available for cross-country skiing and snowshoeing, and it is one of the best trail networks in Maine.

Designed by former Olympian John Morton, the trail system offers a satisfying variety of lengths and difficulties. The 1.4 km Arsenault Pond Loop and 5-km Oak Hill Loop are the easiest, offering gentle slopes and less dramatic corners than the other loops. The other trails offer greater challenges, with steeper grades, and a twisting mix of uphill and downhill traversing. The steepest, the Gloucester Hill Run, even has an orange safety net at the bottom of a pitch to catch errant skiers.

Along with the nice mix of challenges, the variety in scenery is striking. The trails offer a mix of dense, wooded skiing, and wide-open, bright fields. Throughout, you are as likely to spot animal tracks (or the animals themselves) as you are likely to spot another skier.

As a fairly novice Nordic skier, I was struck by the smart choices in design (described to me by more experienced skiers). Pineland's trail system is made up of "stacked" loops, which makes it easy to add or subtract loops for a harder or easier run. The Nordic trails are one-directional, which keeps skiers safe and eases congestion. At every intersection (and in other spots along the trails), signs clearly define where you are on the trails, what is around you, and in which direction you should head. Off-trail, the yurt, Outdoor Center, and warming hut are welcome additions on longer expeditions.

The trails at Pineland are immaculately groomed, as well as any Alpine area in the state. Groomed trails feature both a single-set track for classic skiing and a skate lane for skate skiing.

Along with the Nordic ski trail network, there are almost 20 km of snowshoe trails at Pineland Farms. Most of the trails wind alongside or near the ski trails, covering the terrain north and east of the Outdoor Center. The 8 km Fox Run trail, however, runs south and west of the other trails and offers a bit more privacy. It also skirts alongside the edge of the Pineland Farms buildings on SR 231, providing some interesting visual variety.

Weather permitting, Pineland Farms' trails are open every day from 8 a.m. to 5 p.m. Adult ski and snowshoe passes are available at the Outdoor Center for $13 and $6 a day, respectively, with reduced rates for afternoon tickets. Equipment rentals are available at the Outdoor Center, and private, semiprivate, and group lessons are available by appointment.

If you (or family members) are not interested in skiing or snow-shoeing, Pineland offers a few other recreational opportunities. A giant sledding hill, groomed with Pineland's trail grooming equipment, is open from dawn to dusk. Access to the hill is free, and visitors can either bring their own sleds or rent one from the Outdoor

Center. Pineland's pond is also open for ice skating daily and is free to the public.

If you do choose to visit Pineland to ski or snowshoe, do not miss the Market at Pineland Farms. One of the state's great little locally sourced markets, the shop has mouthwatering produce, meats, cheeses, and baked goods, as well as ready-to-eat food in the deli. After working up an appetite on Pineland's trails, nothing beats their fresh sandwiches and a hot cup of Carrabassett coffee.

Location: New Gloucester
Contact: (207) 688-4800
Price range: Adults $13, children and seniors $9
Trails: 25 km
Available amenities: Rentals, warming hut
Snowshoeing allowed? Yes
Website: http://pinelandfarms.org

RANGELEY LAKES TRAIL CENTER

As you drive up the road to Saddleback Mountain, you will spot the rustic yurt on your left that marks the access point to more than 50 km of superbly groomed and dependably covered cross-country trails that have become the pride of the Rangeley Lakes Region. In addition to the trails are views of the breathtaking western mountain vistas and the surrounding lakes.

Hot and cold beverages, hot soup, and snacks are available in the hut, which also houses the equipment-rental shop. Toward the end of each season, you can even find some great deals on used equipment packages available for sale.

Adults 19 to 64 can use the trails for a full day for $18 or for a half day for $14. For kids 7 to 18, college students, and members of the military, the charge is $10 a day. Seniors over 65 pay $7 a day, and kids under 6 are free.

Should you be an Alpine skier as well, you will find a unique combination option available for a reasonable additional charge on your Saddleback Mountain Ski Area season pass.

The first Sunday of each month (unless it is a holiday) is Maine Day, and Maine resident adults can ski for just $12. Monday is Ladies' Day, with half-price passes and a free cup of soup, and there is a similar deal for men on Tuesday. Wednesday features their buy-one-get-one-free offer, as long as it is not a vacation week.

Each year, one day in January, February, and March is ordained Locals' Appreciation Day, when Rangeley town residents, as well as folks living in Dallas and Sandy River Plantations, ski and rent free!

Rental ski, boot, and pole packages are $13 for adults and $10 for those under 19, college students, members of the military, and seniors. Individual equipment is also available at similarly reasonable rates.

Location: Rangeley
Contact: (207) 864-4309
Price range: Adults $18, children $10, seniors $7
Trails: 67 km
Available amenities: Rentals, warming hut
Snowshoeing allowed? Yes
Website: http://xcskirangeley.com

SPRUCE MOUNTAIN

Spruce Mountain Nordic is located at the base of the Spruce Mountain alpine area, just northwest of the town of Livermore Falls. The small network of trails covers 5 km of terrain, accessible on both Nordic skis and snowshoes.

Food and refreshments are available at the base lodge of the Spruce Mountain alpine area.

It is worth noting, however, that the lodge does not offer rentals—Jay's Ski Depot is the best bet if you do not own your own equipment. Tickets for access to Spruce's XC trail network are available at the resort, as well as at Otis Federal Credit Union in Jay. Daily trail-use fees are $7 for adults and $6 for students.

Location: Jay
Contact: (207) 897-4019
Price range: Adults (including seniors) $7, children $6
Trails: 5 km
Available amenities: Warming hut
Snowshoeing allowed? Yes
Website: www.sprucemountain.org

SUGARLOAF

Billed as Maine's largest Nordic center, and for good reason, this 90 km cross-country behemoth is nestled in the woods right at the foot of Sugarloaf Mountain, the East's biggest ski resort.

In addition to the well-groomed trail network, there is a lodge (renovated in 2007), complete with an NHL-size skating rink. Everything you would expect at a first-class facility is available, from food and drinks to a well-equipped rental shop.

For skiers who have purchased a ticket for the alpine facilities and want to spend a few relaxing hours out touring, their unique Alpine Exchange program lets you ski the slopes and skate the trails in the same day. When you show your ski area lift ticket, the trails are free to you for the rest of the day. Here is the real kicker: You will get free rental equipment as well if you need it! Available anytime between 9 a.m. and 4 p.m.

Adults can access the trails for $21 a day or $16 after 12:30 p.m. The half-day price prevails for multiday tickets. Kids 6 to 12 and seniors 65 to 79 pay $13 for all day and $11 for half-day or multiday tickets. Trail access is free for skiers over 80 or under 5.

The adult (13 to 64) rental package is $21, and after 12:30 p.m. or for multiday use the price drops to $16. For juniors (6 to 12) and seniors (65 to 79), it is $17 for a full day and $13 for half-day or multiday rentals.

Location: Carrabassett Valley
Contact: (207) 237-6830
Price range: Adults $21, children $13, seniors 80+ free
Trails: 90 km
Available amenities: Rentals, warming hut
Snowshoeing allowed? Yes
Website: www.sugarloaf.com

TITCOMB MOUNTAIN NORDIC

Starting right in the base area of Titcomb Mountain Ski Area, there is a 16 km network of trails that generations of Franklin County and other cross-country skiers have both trained on for competitions and cruised recreationally.

The Bog Loop is even lit for evening skiing on the nights that the lifts are operating.

It's open from 3 to 6 p.m. Monday through Thursday, 4 to 8 p.m. Friday, 9 a.m. to 8 p.m. Saturday, and 9 a.m. to 4 p.m. Sunday.

Refreshments and rentals are available right in the base lodge.

For everyone between the ages of 6 and 69, the trail-use fee is just $10. For people under or over those ages, trail use is free.

Bear in mind that trail use is restricted to the times when the lifts are operating, although season pass holders at the ski area can head out on them anytime they want.

Location: West Farmington
Contact: (207) 778-9031
Price range: Age 6–69, $10; children 5 and under and seniors 70 and over, free
Trails: 16 km
Available amenities: Rentals, warming hut
Snowshoeing allowed? Yes
Website: http://titcombmountain.com

NOTABLE MAINE SKIERS

Thousands of Mainers have had an impact on the sport and the business of skiing in their home state. Area developers and operators, coaches, competitors, race officials, equipment innovators, ski patrolmen, and just plain loyal club members and enthusiasts have all left indelible marks on the state's skiing fabric.

It would be impossible to identify and appropriately pay tribute to every one of them, but their contributions are still genuinely appreciated, and we know that the sport we all love and enjoy is more complete because of the impact, large and small, that each of them has contributed.

In an effort to identify and honor those Mainers whose contributions are deemed to have been exceptional, the Ski Museum of Maine created the Maine Ski Hall of Fame in 2003. In the years that have followed, over one hundred distinguished contributors to the sport have been inducted into the Hall of Fame.

The list of future possible entrants is long, and each year new inductees will join the ranks of their fellow honorees.

Complete biographies of Hall of Fame members can be found at www.skimuseumofmaine.org

What follows, by their year of induction, are members through the Class of 2016.

Class of 2003

Robert "Bunny" Bass	Ski boot and ski area pioneer
John Bower	Olympic competitor/Coach
Wendall Broomhall	Olympic competitor/official/course designer
Ralph A. "Doc" Desroches	Area manager/national industry executive

Russ Haggett	Area manager
Aurele Legere	Jumper/jump designer/Olympic official
Wes Marco	Instructor/examiner
C. Allison Merrill	College coach
Otto Walling	Area founder/manager

Class of 2004

Donald Cross	Area developer/grooming pioneer
Linwood "Zeke" Dwelley	Coach
Paul Kailey	Area founder/coach/shop owner
Jean Luce	Club official/race organizer/museum founder
Birger Olsen	Competitor/promoter
Sam Ouelet	Cross-country competitor and champion
Roger Page	Instructor/ski school director/area developer
Tom Reynolds	Instructor/coach/innovator
Greg Stump	Freestyle champion/moviemaker
Robert "Stub" Taylor	Patrol director/examiner

Class of 2005

Karl Anderson	Olympian
Franklin Emery	Patrolman/race official/wax maker
Theo Johnsen	Ski maker/author
James "Jimmy" Jones	Patrol director/certifier/coach
Dick and Mary Kendall	Race officials and organizers/ instructors/coaches
Robert Morse	Coach
Richard "Pat" Murphy	Patrolman
Richard "Dick" Osgood	Competitor/coach
Robert Pidacks	Olympian/coach
Robert "Rem" Remington	Competitor/coach

Class of 2006

Charles Akers	Olympian/patrolman
Ray Broomhall	Competitor/coach
Fletcher Brown	Instructor/ski area director
John Christie	Patrolman/area manager, developer and owner/author
Norm Cummings	Competitor/coach/jumping judge
Dick Gould	Competitor/coach/instructor
Irv Kagan	Freestyle innovator/official
Jack Lufkin	Olympian/ski school director/ shop manager
George Ouellette	Broadcaster/journalist/ Olympic announcer
Peter Webber	Competitor/shop owner/ area executive

Class of 2007

Richard "Dick" Bell	Industry pioneer and promoter/ area director
Charles "Slim" Broomhall	Competitor/coach/Olympic official
Bob Flynn	Coach/race organizer/rules official
Dave Irons	Patrolman/journalist
Jim Miller	Olympian/coach
Winsten "Win" Robbins	Lift engineer and pioneer/ safety inspector
Galen Sayward	Competitor/coach/Olympic official
Murray "Mike" Thurston	Area founder/director

Class of 2008

Leslie Bancroft	World Cup competitor
Bill Cummings	Competitor/NCAA official
H. King Cummings	Area president/industry visionary
Hans Jenni	Ski school director
Robert C. Kendall	Olympian
Tim LaVallee	Competitor/coach

Pat Miller	Olympian
Julie Parisien	Olympian/World Cup winner
Dan Simoneau	Three-time Olympian

Class of 2009

Herbert L. "Herb" Adams	Competitor/coach/race official
Tom Bennett	Patrolman/club and race organizer/ official
Sarah Billmeier	Three-time Paralympics Gold Medalist
Ted Curtis	Coach
Byron "Bud" Dow	Instructor/area developer/ race organizer
John Litchfield	Competitor/ski school director/ area developer
Les Otten	Area developer, operator, owner
John Roderick	Competitor/race official/coach

Class of 2010

John Atwood	Competitor/coach
Kirsten Clark-Rickenbach	Olympian/coach
Joan McWilliams Dolan	National Freestyle Champion/coach
Bob Harkins	Patrolman/coach/area executive
Morten Lund	Journalist/historian
Marcus Nash	Olympian/coach
Bernard Paradis	Coach/area operations

Class of 2011

Horace Chapman	Area pioneer/director
Chip Crothers	Handicapped Skiing founder
David Farrar	Competitor/judge/patrolman
John Greene	Olympian/equipment innovator
Edmund MacDonald	Journalist
Carla Marcus	Safety expert/WinterKids director
Werner Rothbacher	Ski school director/coach
Owen Wells	Philanthropist/area developer

Class of 2012

L.L.Bean	Promoter/equipment and clothing pioneer/retailer
Andre Benoit	Instructor/retailer
Erlon "Bucky" Broomhal	Competitor/coach
Bruce Fenn	Instructor/ski school director/coach
Frank Howell	Freestyle innovator/coach/judge
Philip Hussey	Ski jump and lift builder/ area developer
Walter Stadig	Competitor/lift inventor/ area developer
Natalie Terry	Instructor

Class of 2013

Gail Blackburn	US Ski Team member
Brice Cole	Competitor/instructor/coach
Will Farnham	Ski Patrol organizer/coach/ race official
Craig Gray	Paralympian/US Disabled Ski Team
Randy Kerr	US Ski Team member
Howard Paradis	Competitor/coach
Greg Poirier	Competitor/Olympic Team coach/ USSA executive
Rand Stowell	Industry pioneer/area director

Class of 2014

Bill Briggs	Instructor/extreme-skiing pioneer
Carl Burnett	Paralympic competitor
Dave Carter	Competitor/Nordic center developer
Brud Folger	Competitor/college coach
Tom Gyger	Patrolman
Rob and Anna Parisien	Brother and sister Olympians
Nikki Pilavakis-Davoren	Boarder cross champion

Class of 2015

Bruce Chalmers	Competitor and coach, junior skiing program organizer
Peter Davis	US Nordic Ski Team member, coach
John Diller	Freestyle coach and innovator, ski area executive
Tom Kendall	Competitor, timing-technology innovator
Luba Lowery	US Disabled Olympic Team, National Champion, coach
Jill Sickels Matlock	Competitor and coach, US Extreme Skiing Champion
John Ritzo	Former Headmaster at Carrabassett Valley Academy
Megan Roberts	Competitor, coach and area manager

Class of 2016

Nancy Fiddler	Olympic cross-country team member
Sonny Goodwin	Ski area builder
Ed Rogers	Ski resort entrepreneur, pro-racing producer
Andrew Shepard	Revitalized two ski areas, developed youth programs
Walt Shepard	US National biathlon team medal winner
Geoff Stump	Freestyle competitor, coach, filmmaker
Greg Sweetser	Area marketing executive, Trade Association Director
Dan Warner	Four event competitor, official

LOST SKI AREAS

During the halcyon decades between the 1940s and 1970s, scores of ski areas of all sorts and sizes were in operation from one corner of Maine to the other.

Most were small rope-tow-served mom-and-pop, community, and club operations. Others were more substantial, with surface cable lifts; still others were larger facilities with aerial lifts; and a few qualified as major development projects with multiple cable lifts and expansive base lodges.

Some eighty fell into the dust bin of history, and the reasons were as varied as the facilities. Energy and insurance costs did some in, while others suffered from lack of snow or flagging utilization. Even more closed when larger areas were developed and their clientele opted for the terrain, lifts, and amenities offered by the newcomers.

Despite the reduced number of ski areas, and the fact that not a single new alpine area has been launched in the state in over forty years, skiing today in Maine is still a vibrant industry, employing thousands, contributing to local economies, and entertaining throngs of Mainers and folks from away.

The list of ski areas below is testimony to the spirit of our forebears who did so much, with so little, for so many, to launch the sport and industry.

The information that follows is derived in great part from the work of the New England Lost Ski Areas Project. A visit to their website, www.nelsap.org, can be a rewarding experience as it contains a treasure trove of information about virtually every lost area. This is an interactive site, so if you can fill in some blanks or have information about a particular area that has been overlooked or erroneously reported, you are welcome to chime in.

Ski Areas along the Coast and 30 Miles Inland

Alden's Hill	Gorham
Bald Mountain	Dedham
Bauneg Beg	North Berwick
Bauneg Beg Ski Trails	North Berwick
Beaver Hill	Sanford
Belfast	Belfast
Bell Slope	Lewiston
Big Hill	East Holden
Cumberland	Cumberland
Deer Hill	Westbrook
Dundee Heights	North Gorham
Dutton Hill Ski Area	Windham
Eastport Ski Area	Pembroke
Essex Street Hill	Bangor
Gorham Kiwanis	Gorham
Hillside	Monroe
Hurricane Ski Slope	Falmouth
Kimball's Hill	Kennebunk
King's Mountain Slope	Bangor
Maggie's Mountain	Freeport
Maple Hill Slope	Sinclair
McFarland Slope	Bar Harbor
Mount Agamenticus	York
Mount Gile	East Auburn
Oak Grove School	Vassalboro
Paradise Park	Bangor
Pine Haven	Lewiston
Ski-Horse	Newburgh
Sky Hy Park	Topsham
Snow Mountain	Winterport

Spring Hill	South Berwick
Stultz Tow	West Falmouth
Sunrise Ski Slope	Alexander
Veazie	Veazie

Central Maine Ski Areas

Bijah	Starks
Colby College	Waterville
Dexter	Dexter
Dunham's Mtn. Farm	Waterville
Gilmour's Hill	Winthrop
Guilford Kiwanis	Guilford
Hebron Academy	Hebron
Hi Point Tow	Augusta
Hobb's Hill	Harrison
Hotham's Slope	Auburn
Maine Top Ski Tow	Augusta
Mount Quito	Casco
No-Par Ski Area	Norway
Norway-Paris Outing Club	Norway-Paris
Oxford Hills High School (Ben Barrows Hill)	Hebron
Poland Spring	Poland Spring
Sand Hill	Augusta
Silver Hills	Chelsea
Western View	Augusta

Western and Northern Maine

Bald Mountain	Oquossoc
Black Cat	Millinocket
Bond Mountain	Newfield
Burnt Meadow Mountain	Brownfield
County Tow	Fort Kent
Evergreen Valley	Stoneham
Enchanted Mtn.	Jackman
Gould Academy	Bethel
Hathaway's	Medway
Hiram (exact name unknown)	Hiram
Jockey Cap	Fryeburg
Lincoln Municipal	Lincoln
Lone Mountain	Andover
Loring AFB	Limestone
Manor Hill	Rangeley
Maple Grove	Sinclair
May Mountain	Island Falls
Mount Carmel	Madawaska
Northmen	Caribou
Prestile	Caribou
Scottie's	Rumford
Ski-W (Starks Hill)	Fryeburg
Spruce Street Tow	Rumford
Van Buren Ski Way	Keegan
White Bunny	Fort Fairfield

ACKNOWLEDGMENTS

This book could not have been written without the generous support of the Ski Maine Association and the enthusiastic endorsement and assistance from its Executive Director, Greg Sweetser.

Individual member areas of the association, both Alpine and Nordic, provided important background material and priceless photographs, along with their hospitality, which allowed both of us to explore the nooks and crannies of their facilities.

Important historical information was gleaned from *First Tracks: Stories From Maine's Skiing Heritage*, published in 1995 by the Ski Maine Association and authored by Glenn Parkinson, Maine's foremost ski historian and past president of both the Ski Museum of Maine and the New England Ski Museum. This book proved to be a treasure trove of information about the origins of skiing in Maine as a sport and as an industry, and provided insight into the history of both past and present ski areas.

We are grateful to Bruce Miles, Executive Director of the Ski Museum of Maine, for providing information about Maine's notable skiers from the Maine Ski Hall of Fame archives.

The New England Lost Ski Areas Project (NELSAP), rendered important details about nearly eighty ski areas that once operated in Maine but, for a variety of reasons, are now only memories. We were saved hundreds of research hours thanks to NELSAP's compilation and historical data about each area.

Both of our wives proved to be ever-patient and understanding as we conducted research on countless days and weekends out on our skis: research which, to both of us, never even came close to fitting the definition of "work."

INDEX

Page numbers preceded by *insert* refer to photo insert section.

ABOUT THE AUTHORS

John Christie is a member of the Maine Ski Hall of Fame and past president of the Ski Museum of Maine. He has served as general manager of both Sugarloaf/USA in Maine and Mt. Snow in Vermont. He was also owner of Saddleback Mountain in Maine and a president of the Vermont Ski Areas Association. He served on the board of the National Ski Areas Association. John is the author of *The Story of Sugarloaf*, coauthor with Josh of the *Maine Outdoor Adventure Guide*, and also contributed to *Atlantic Coastal Kayaker* magazine and *Maine Seniors* magazine, as well as the *Maine Sunday Telegram*. He lived in Washington, Maine, until his death in 2016.

Josh Christie has written and contributed to a number of works of nonfiction, including *Maine Beer: Brewing in Vacationland*, the *Maine Outdoor Adventure Guide*, and *Read This*. He is a regular contributor to the *Maine Sunday Telegram* and is a former board member of the eastern chapter of the North American Snow Sports Journalists Association. Josh lives on Maine's southern coast and manages an independent bookstore in Portland, Maine.